OPPOSING
VIEWPOINTS®
SERIES

Cars in America

Other Books of Related Interest:

Opposing Viewpoints Series

Energy Alternatives

At Issue Series

Ethanol

Current Controversies Series

Pollution

"Congress shall make
no law . . . abridging
the freedom of speech,
or of the press."

First Amendment to the U.S. Constitution

The basic foundation of our democracy is the First Amendment guarantee of freedom of expression. The Opposing Viewpoints Series is dedicated to the concept of this basic freedom and the idea that it is more important to practice it than to enshrine it.

Cars in America

Roman Espejo, Book Editor

GREENHAVEN PRESS
A part of Gale, Cengage Learning

GALE
CENGAGE Learning™

Detroit • New York • San Francisco • New Haven, Conn • Waterville, Maine • London

Christine Nasso, *Publisher*
Elizabeth Des Chenes, *Managing Editor*

© 2010 Greenhaven Press, a part of Gale, Cengage Learning.

Gale and Greenhaven Press are registered trademarks used herein under license.

For more information, contact:
Greenhaven Press
27500 Drake Rd.
Farmington Hills, MI 48331-3535
Or you can visit our Internet site at gale.cengage.com

For product information and technology assistance, contact us at

Gale Customer Support, 1-800-877-4253
For permission to use material from this text or product, submit all requests online at www.cengage.com/permissions

Further permissions questions can be emailed to permissionrequest@cengage.com

Articles in Greenhaven Press anthologies are often edited for length to meet page requirements. In addition, original titles of these works are changed to clearly present the main thesis and to explicitly indicate the author's opinion. Every effort is made to ensure that Greenhaven Press accurately reflects the original intent of the authors. Every effort has been made to trace the owners of copyrighted material.

Cover Image copyright Comstock Images/Getty Images.

LIBRARY OF CONGRESS CATALOGING-IN-PUBLICATION DATA

Cars in America / Roman Espejo, book editor.
     p. cm. -- (Opposing viewpoints)
  Includes bibliographical references and index.
  ISBN 978-0-7377-4759-1 (hardcover) -- ISBN 978-0-7377-4760-7 (pbk.)
  1. Automobile industry and trade--United States--Juvenile literature.
  2. Automobiles--Social aspects--United States--Juvenile literature.
  3. Transportation--United States--Juvenile literature. I. Espejo, Roman, 1977-
  HD9710.U52C267 2010
  388.3'210973--dc22

                                                                    2009050444

Printed in the United States of America
2 3 4 5 6 7 14 13 12 11 10

Contents

Chapter 3: What Is the Future of the Car Industry in America?

Chapter 4: How Can the United States Meet Its Future Transportation Needs?

Why Consider
Opposing Viewpoints?

> *"The only way in which a human being can make some approach to knowing the whole of a subject is by hearing what can be said about it by persons of every variety of opinion and studying all modes in which it can be looked at by every character of mind. No wise man ever acquired his wisdom in any mode but this."*
>
> John Stuart Mill

In our media-intensive culture it is not difficult to find differing opinions. Thousands of newspapers and magazines and dozens of radio and television talk shows resound with differing points of view. The difficulty lies in deciding which opinion to agree with and which "experts" seem the most credible. The more inundated we become with differing opinions and claims, the more essential it is to hone critical reading and thinking skills to evaluate these ideas. Opposing Viewpoints books address this problem directly by presenting stimulating debates that can be used to enhance and teach these skills. The varied opinions contained in each book examine many different aspects of a single issue. While examining these conveniently edited opposing views, readers can develop critical thinking skills such as the ability to compare and contrast authors' credibility, facts, argumentation styles, use of persuasive techniques, and other stylistic tools. In short, the Opposing Viewpoints Series is an ideal way to attain the higher-level thinking and reading skills so essential in a culture of diverse and contradictory opinions.

In addition to providing a tool for critical thinking, Opposing Viewpoints books challenge readers to question their own strongly held opinions and assumptions. Most people form their opinions on the basis of upbringing, peer pressure, and personal, cultural, or professional bias. By reading carefully balanced opposing views, readers must directly confront new ideas as well as the opinions of those with whom they disagree. This is not to simplistically argue that everyone who reads opposing views will—or should—change his or her opinion. Instead, the series enhances readers' understanding of their own views by encouraging confrontation with opposing ideas. Careful examination of others' views can lead to the readers' understanding of the logical inconsistencies in their own opinions, perspective on why they hold an opinion, and the consideration of the possibility that their opinion requires further evaluation.

Evaluating Other Opinions

To ensure that this type of examination occurs, Opposing Viewpoints books present all types of opinions. Prominent spokespeople on different sides of each issue as well as well-known professionals from many disciplines challenge the reader. An additional goal of the series is to provide a forum for other, less known, or even unpopular viewpoints. The opinion of an ordinary person who has had to make the decision to cut off life support from a terminally ill relative, for example, may be just as valuable and provide just as much insight as a medical ethicist's professional opinion. The editors have two additional purposes in including these less known views. One, the editors encourage readers to respect others' opinions—even when not enhanced by professional credibility. It is only by reading or listening to and objectively evaluating others' ideas that one can determine whether they are worthy of consideration. Two, the inclusion of such viewpoints encourages the important critical thinking skill of objectively evaluating an author's credentials and bias. This evaluation will illuminate an author's reasons for taking a particular stance on an issue and will aid in readers' evaluation of the author's ideas.

It is our hope that these books will give readers a deeper understanding of the issues debated and an appreciation of the complexity of even seemingly simple issues when good and honest people disagree. This awareness is particularly important in a democratic society such as ours in which people enter into public debate to determine the common good. Those with whom one disagrees should not be regarded as enemies but rather as people whose views deserve careful examination and may shed light on one's own.

Thomas Jefferson once said that "difference of opinion leads to inquiry, and inquiry to truth." Jefferson, a broadly educated man, argued that "if a nation expects to be ignorant and free . . . it expects what never was and never will be." As individuals and as a nation, it is imperative that we consider the opinions of others and examine them with skill and discernment. The Opposing Viewpoints Series is intended to help readers achieve this goal.

David L. Bender and Bruno Leone,
Founders

Introduction

> "*I strongly believe hydrogen is the fuel of the future.*"[1]
>
> —*George W. Bush,*
> *forty-third president of the United States*
>
> "*Hydrogen is not a magical new source of energy.*"[2]
>
> —*Vijay V. Vaitheeswaran,*
> *global correspondent of the* Economist

In May 2009, President Barack Obama eliminated the $1.2 billion plan for hydrogen fuel cell development introduced by former president George W. Bush, whose administration had spent $500 million on such research. Six years earlier, Bush announced the Hydrogen Fuel Initiative (HFI) in his State of the Union address. The objective of the HFI was to bring the hydrogen car into reality by 2020, bolstered by the Energy Policy Act (EPAct) of 2005 and the Advanced Energy Initiative (AEI) of 2006.

Steven Chu, Obama's secretary of energy, recommended the budgetary cutback. He maintained that the infrastructure to fuel hydrogen cars would cost billions, and efforts should focus on available green technologies. "We asked ourselves, 'Is it likely in the next 10 or 15, 20 years that we will convert to a hydrogen car economy?' The answer, we felt, was 'no,'"[3] Chu said in a briefing. Additionally, in an interview for *Technology Review*, the Nobel Prize–winning physicist famously proclaimed that making more efficient, less expensive fuel cells and dramatically improving the production, transportation, and storage of hydrogen would be nearly impossible: "If you need four miracles, that's unlikely: Saints only need three miracles."[4]

The same month, Mary Nichols, chair of the California Air Resources Board (CARB), spoke with Chu in person about his position on hydrogen and fuel cell technology. Nichols followed up the meeting with a letter, in which she responded to Chu's claims. "Hydrogen and fuel cells show great potential and have met or exceeded nearly all of the technical milestones set out by the U.S. DOE [Department of Energy]." Nichols continued, stating that "the market will decide which technologies are the winners, but given the critical importance to our long-term climate and energy security goals, the best approach is to pursue and invest in a portfolio of the most promising options."[5] For instance, she asserted that in California production of hydrogen cars would reach about fifty thousand by 2017.

Fuel cells work by converting hydrogen and oxygen into water, which creates electricity. Their by-products are water and heat. In 1800, British scientists first used electricity to separate water into its elements, hydrogen and oxygen. Thirty-eight years later, Welsh physicist William Robert Grove created the first fuel cell by achieving a continuous flow of electricity between electrodes in containers of hydrogen and oxygen and sulfuric acid. After being modified by General Electric (GE) researchers, Willard Thomas Grubb in 1955 and Leonard Niedrach in 1958, the "Grubb-Niedrach" fuel cell was used by the National Aeronautics and Space Administration (NASA) in the Gemini space project in the mid-1960s.

The first commercially viable hydrogen motor vehicle appeared in 1993, when Canadian company Ballard Power Systems took to the Vancouver streets with a bus powered by fuel cells. At an auto show in 2005, General Motors (GM) debuted its fuel cell car, the Sequel, scheduled for production in 2010. In 2008, Honda introduced its own, the FCX Clarity. As of October 2009, the model is available on very limited lease in the area of Los Angeles, California, home to over a dozen hydrogen filling stations. Also, Daimler and Hyundai have plans to begin mass production of hydrogen automobiles in 2012.

Proponents stress that fuel cells and hydrogen offer key benefits over conventional gas and gas-electric hybrid engines. They insist that hydrogen fuel promises to be very low or zero-emissions once the technology is perfected, negating both the environmental impacts of fossil fuels and reliance on foreign oil. "Knowing how to integrate these new technologies into existing lifestyles and then building new infrastructures to make it work is the trick," states Stephen Ellis, manager of fuel cell marketing for Honda and FCX Clarity leasing in Torrance, California. "It took a hundred years to create the gasoline infrastructure; this will be much faster."[6]

Opponents, on the other hand, concur with Steven Chu's concerns. The late Alex Farrell, an energy expert and associate professor at the University of California, Berkeley, alleged that hydrogen cars are cost prohibitive: "The real number we have to pay attention to is half a million to a million dollars a car."[7] Julio Friedmann, head of the Carbon Management Program for Lawrence Livermore National Laboratory, contends that the fuel cell will not revolutionize transportation. "People changed from horses to gasoline cars because they got a huge improvement in their lives," says Friedmann. "Changing from gasoline to hydrogen doesn't get you that, necessarily."[8] And Patrick Bedard, editor-at-large of *Car and Driver*, alleges that hydrogen fuel, in the big picture, may not be cleaner after all because it takes energy to create it. "As for global-warming implications, the use of hydrogen from coal instead of gasoline would produce a 2.7-fold increase in carbon emissions,"[9] he argues.

In October 2009, the U.S. Senate reinstated almost all of the federal funding Obama had cut from hydrogen fuel cell development. "It's the right set of priorities," claims Byron L. Dorgan, a North Dakota senator and advocate of fuel cells. "If you discontinue the research, you shortchange the future."[10] However, Joseph J. Romm, a former Department of Energy official, disagrees with the decision: "It's an insult to the

American taxpayer to pretend that hydrogen cars are a practical and affordable near-term or even medium-term greenhouse gas reduction strategy."[11]

The debate over the hydrogen fuel cell covers some of the most pressing issues relating to cars: carbon emissions, oil dependence, the automobile industry crisis, and the country's transportation needs. *Opposing Viewpoints: Cars in America* probes these and other topics in the following chapters: How Do Cars Affect Life in the United States? How Can Driving in America Be Made Safer? What Is the Future of the Car Industry in America? and How Can the United States Meet Its Future Transportation Needs? From varying platforms and positions, the authors connect life on the road to social, economic, and environmental well-being of the nation.

Notes

1. April 22, 2006. http://query.nytimes.com.
2. *Nieman Reports*, Summer 2004. www.nieman.harvard.edu.
3. Grist.com, May 8, 2009. www.grist.org.
4. *Technology Review*, May 14, 2009. www.technologyreview.com.
5. Greencarcongress.com, June 19, 2009. www.greencarcongress.com.
6. *TIME*, September 2, 2009. www.time.com.
7. Abc7news.com, April 1, 2008. http://abclocal.go.com.
8. Abc7news.com, April 1, 2008. http://abclocal.go.com.
9. *Car and Driver*, October 2005. www.caranddriver.com.
10. *Washington Post*, October 17, 2009. www.washingtonpost.com.
11. *Washington Post*, October 17, 2009. www.washingtonpost.com.

CHAPTER 1

How Do Cars Affect Life in the United States?

Chapter Preface

"America is addicted to oil, which is often imported from unstable parts of the world,"[1] declared former president George W. Bush in his State of the Union speech on January 31, 2006. His remarks referenced both the country's dependence on the oil-rich Middle East and three-year-long Iraq War. Also, drivers use almost 70 percent of the 21 million barrels consumed daily by the nation, according to the National Commission on Energy. Global consumption is estimated to be 85 million barrels a day.

Looking to alternative fuels and hybrid and electric cars, Bush stated that the objective is to reduce America's oil imports from the region by more than 75 percent by 2025. "By applying the talent and technology of America," he continued, "this country can dramatically improve our environment, move beyond a petroleum-based economy, and make our dependence on Middle Eastern oil a thing of the past."[2]

Two years later, during the summer of 2008, oil prices reached $4 a gallon. While cash-strapped Americans had no choice but to cut down on driving, critics argued that the United States must end its love affair with the automobile. Retired New Mexico senator Pete Domenici, who served on the Senate Energy and Natural Resources Committee, claims, "We've got to fix it or our standard of living will change within a decade. Oil was too damn cheap, it's too high now and it's going even higher."[3]

Other observers, however, insist that America is not addicted to oil. Alex Epstein, analyst for the Ayn Rand Institute, argues, "We are not 'addicted' to oil any more than we are 'addicted' to the myriad values it makes possible, like fresh food, imported electronics, going to work, or visiting loved ones."[4] In addition, political commentator Daniel Lapin counters Bush's arguments for energy independence from the

Middle East, stating, "The serious problem is not that we import oil from unstable countries. The problem is that it is more expensive than we'd like."[5] Lapin suggests that some solutions are to drill for more oil in Alaska and help Canada develop its supposed reserves. In the following chapter, the authors debate whether car culture has shaped America for better or worse.

Notes

1. C-SPAN. www.cspan.org.
2. C-SPAN. www.cspan.org.
3. Nelson D. Schwartz, *New York Times*, July 6, 2008.
4. Aynrand.org, July 6, 2006. www.aynrand.org.
5. *Orthodoxy Today*, February 4, 2006. www.orthodoxytoday .org.

VIEWPOINT 1

| *"America's all-consuming love affair with the car is fading."*

Car Culture Harms Americans

Paul Harris

Paul Harris is a U.S. correspondent for the Guardian. *In the following viewpoint, Harris claims that America's car culture is heading toward a fundamental change: Because of prohibitively high oil prices, the automobile is losing its practical and symbolic value, becoming an unsustainable burden to both drivers and dwellers of suburbia. He asserts that plummeting sales of large, fuel-inefficient cars—particularly sport utility vehicles (SUVs)—threaten to collapse the American auto industry. Furthermore, Harris warns that as Americans shift away from car-centered lifestyles, the nation's once-tranquil suburbs will transform into crime-ridden areas of unemployment and blight.*

As you read, consider the following questions:

1. According to the author, how is bicycle culture changing in southern California?

2. What customs are spreading among Americans in efforts to drive less, as stated by Harris?

3. In Harris's view, why have small towns and rural areas been hit the hardest by the rising cost of oil?

It is known as the Inland Empire: a vast stretch of land tucked in the high desert valleys east of Los Angeles. Once home to fruit trees and Indians, it is now a concrete sprawl of jammed freeways, endless suburbs and shopping malls.

But here, in the heartland of the four-wheel drive, a revolution is under way. What was once unthinkable is becoming a shocking reality: America's all-consuming love affair with the car is fading.

Surging petrol prices have worked where environmental arguments have failed. Many Americans have long been told to cut back on car use. Now [summer 2008], facing $4-a-gallon fuel, they have no choice.

Take Adam Garcia, a security guard who works near the railway station in Riverside. Like many Inland Empire residents, he commutes a huge distance: 100 miles a day. He used to think nothing of it. But now, faced with petrol costs that have tripled, he is taking action. He has even altered the engine of his car to boost its mileage. 'I have to. Everyone does. I can't afford to drive as much as I did,' he said.

Recent figures showed the steepest monthly drop in miles driven by Americans since 1942. At the same time car sales are collapsing, led by huge SUVs [sport utility vehicles].

General Motors [GM], once the very image of American industrial might, is in deep trouble. Cities are now investing in mass transit, hoping to tempt people back into town centres from far-flung commuter belts where they are now stranded by high petrol prices.

Jonathan Baty used to be a pioneer. The lighting designer has cycled to work every day since 1993. It's a nine-mile round trip through the heartland of a car-based culture once famously termed 'Autopia'. But now Baty has company on his daily rides as others choose two wheels rather than four to navigate southern California's streets. 'We have seen a whole emergence of a bike culture in this area. There is a crescendo of interest,' said Baty, who does volunteer work for a cycling group, Bicycle Commuter Coalition of the Inland Empire.

In Riverside, bus travel is up 12 percent on a year ago, rising to 40 percent on commuter routes. Use of the town's railway link is up eight percent. A local carpooling system is up 40 percent. It is the same in the rest of the US. In South Florida a light rail system has reported a 28 percent jump in passengers. In Philadelphia one has shown an 11 percent rise. Even nationwide scooter sales have shot up. At the same time car sales are hitting 15-year record lows. Last week [in July 2008] major American carmakers reported a devastating 18 percent drop in car sales.

A More Fundamental Shift

The numbers point to a more fundamental shift. In America car sales carry a symbolic value that transcends the wheeler-dealering of the showroom. This is a nation of fabled road trips and Route 66. 'There is an American dream of mobility and freedom and wealth. The car is part of all that,' said Professor Michael Dear, an urban studies expert at the University of Southern California.

In the 1950s the confident nation that helped win the Second World War was expressed in classic car designs of huge fins and open tops. By the 1990s it had become the HUMMER, a huge bulking car born from the military. Now there is to be another shift. For, hidden within the car sales figures, is a more complex story than a simple fall. Sales of big cars are plummeting while smaller vehicles, especially fuel-efficient hybrids, are replacing them.

GM has now closed SUV production at four plants. Its HUMMER brand is up for sale, or might even be closed. GM is ploughing huge resources into its 2010 launch of the Chevy Volt, a hybrid car that may get up to 150 miles a gallon. It needs to. GM's share price recently hit a 54-year low, prompting one top investment bank to warn that the firm could go bankrupt [General Motors did enter bankruptcy in 2009].

The Volt, and cars like it, could become symbols of a new more conservation-minded car age. As Americans enjoyed the 4 July holiday weekend, increasing numbers of them were staying at home rather than hitting the road. Newspapers were full of tips for 'staycations', not weekend breaks away. Customs once scorned, such as carpooling and cutting out trips to the mall, are now commonplace. The fact is the vast majority of Americans cannot give up their cars altogether. Too many cities lack any reliable public transport.

Adam Garcia is one of those caught. He does two jobs and his daily road trip by car is a necessity. 'We don't have much of a choice. I have to drive,' he said. Sacrifices come elsewhere, in giving up trips to the cinema and to see friends.

But America's changing relationship with the car is just part of the story of how the most powerful nation is changing in the face of the oil price rise. America has been built on an oil-based economy, from its office workers in the suburbs to its farmers in the fields.

Since the 1950s and the building of the pioneering car-orientated suburb of Levittown in Long Island, the American city has been designed for the convenience of the car as much as its human inhabitants. People live miles away from jobs, shops or entertainment. If you take away cars, the entire suburban way of life collapses. To some, that development is long overdue.

'Suburbia has been unsustainable since its creation,' said Chris Fauchere, a Denver-based filmmaker who is producing a new documentary on the issue called *The Great Squeeze*. 'It was created around cheap oil. People thought it would flow easily from the earth forever.'

Fauchere's film, due out later this year, aims to tackle the profound changes caused by a world where oil is becoming scarcer. He does not think that it is going to be easy for America to make the adjustment. 'It is going to be tough. It is like a chain reaction through the economy. But if you look at history, it is only crisis that starts change,' he said.

The suburbs are already being hit. As cars become more expensive, the justification for suburbs seems to disappear. Some commentators have even suggested that suburbs—once the archetype of an ideal American life—will become the new slums.

The New Inner Cities

In the face of expensive fuel and crashing property prices, the one-time embodiment of a certain American dream will become crime-ridden, dotted by empty lots and home to the poor and unemployed. That is already happening as crime and gang violence has risen in many suburban areas and tens of thousands of homes have been repossessed because of the mortgage crisis.

In effect, suburbs will become the new inner cities, even as once-abandoned American downtowns are undergoing a remarkable renaissance. Even malls, the ultimate symbol of American life since the war, are undergoing a crisis as consumers start to stay away.

But there are even deeper changes going on. The car, the freeway system and cheap air travel made America smaller. Everywhere was easily accessible. That, too, is ending. Higher fuel prices have dealt a terrible blow to America's airlines. They are slashing flights, raising costs and abandoning routes. Some small cities are now losing their air connections.

In effect, America is becoming larger again. That will lead to a more localised economy. To many environmentalists that is a blessing, not a curse. They point out that cheap fuel for industrial transport has meant the average packaged salad has travelled 1,500 miles before it gets to a supermarket shelf.

Choking on Car Culture

In the 1940s, smoking was packaged and sold in advertisements displaying Santa Claus bringing Christmas cheer with a pack of Camels. Who would have thought that 50 years later we'd have local governments banning smoking in bars, parks and even your own apartment? Like cigarettes, once a symbol of sex and sophistication, cars have long been the cherished object of status, wealth and independence, a prized possession among Americans. And just like with cigarettes, we are slowly starting to choke on car culture.

But the surgeon general's alert on smoking wasn't enough to overcome smokers who were already hooked; so why would rising gas prices and global warming permanently void our devotion to cars? It took decades of grassroots campaigns and anti-cigarette movements to reverse the common perception of smoking. It will probably take the same for driving. Green guilt will only carry the environmentally minded driver so far. And commuter checks aren't enough to push the lightweight commuter over the edge.

Erin Sherbert, "Fueling the Fire,"
Metroactive, December 12, 2007.

'Distance is now an enemy,' said Professor Bill McKibben, author of the 1989 climate-change classic *The End of Nature*. 'There's no question that the days of thoughtless driving are done.'

The worst hit parts of the US are not yet the suburbs or the freeways of southern California, but the small towns that dot the Great Plains, Appalachia and the rural Deep South. Even more than the Inland Empire, people in these isolated and poor areas are reliant on cheap petrol and much less able to afford the new prices at the pump. Stories abound of agricultural workers unable to afford to get to the fields and of rural businesses going bust.

Even farmers are not immune. They might not need a car to get to their fields but their fertilisers use oil-based products whose prices have gone through the roof. A handful have started using horses again for some tasks, saving petrol on farm vehicles.

The American dream of the last half century is thus changing. The car and its culture [are] now under a pressure unimaginable even a few years ago. 'The frontier of endless mobility that we've known our entire lives is closing,' said McKibben.

America's excess has had many imitators. Recently a delegation of Chinese government officials and architects visited an Arizona suburb near Phoenix. Approving notes were taken as they surveyed the luxurious car-driven suburban lifestyle on display. This was just one of the many delegations that regularly come from the Far East or South America.

Even as America is sobering up from its excess of cheap oil, other parts of the world are seeking to join the party. They, too, want homes far from dirty city centres, huge open roads and fast cars. It is still a beguiling vision of freedom, mobility and bountiful riches.

McKibben spent last week on a visit to Beijing. He was worried about what he saw. Even as America's obsession with the car lifestyle is ending, others are embracing it. 'The Chinese have spent the Bush years starting to build their own version of America. A key question for the planet is whether they still have time to build a version of Europe instead—global warming will probably hinge on the answer to that question,' he said.

> "The anti-suburbs culture has also fostered many myths about sprawl and driving, a few of which deserve to be reconsidered."

The Harms of Car Culture Are Myths

Ted Balaker and Sam Staley

In the following viewpoint, Ted Balaker and Sam Staley challenge the main arguments against the automobile and its impacts on life in the United States. They assert that Americans are no more dependent on driving than their city-dwelling counterparts, and mass transit is a limited solution to traffic congestion. Also, Balaker and Staley say that air quality has actually improved due to technological advances, and suburban development is not encroaching the country's open spaces. Finally, driving less in America to meet emissions standards would not halt global warming, the authors maintain. Balaker and Staley are co-authors of The Road More Traveled: Why the Congestion Crisis Matters More than You Think, and What We Can Do About It.

As you read, consider the following questions:

1. How do Balaker and Staley describe Americans' views of Europeans and driving?

2. How should mass transit be improved, according to the authors?

3. In the authors' opinion, how would drastically restricting carbon dioxide emissions affect the poor in America and worldwide?

They don't rate up there with cancer and al Qaeda—at least not yet—but suburban sprawl and automobiles are rapidly acquiring a reputation as scourges of modern American society. Sprawl, goes the typical indictment, devours open space, exacerbates global warming and causes pollution, social alienation and even obesity. And cars are the evil co-conspirator—the driving force, so to speak, behind sprawl.

Yet the anti-suburbs culture has also fostered many myths about sprawl and driving, a few of which deserve to be reconsidered:

1. Americans Are Addicted to Driving

Actually, Americans aren't addicted to their cars any more than office workers are addicted to their computers. Both items are merely tools that allow people to accomplish tasks faster and more conveniently. The New York metropolitan area is home to the nation's most extensive transit system, yet even there it takes transit riders about twice as long as drivers to get to work.

In 1930, the interstate highway system and the rise of suburbia were still decades away, and yet car ownership was already widespread, with three in four households having an automobile. Look at any U.S. city and the car is the dominant mode of travel.

Some claim that Europeans have developed an enlightened alternative. Americans return from London and Paris and tell their friends that everyone gets around by transit. But tourists tend to confine themselves to the central cities. Europeans may enjoy top-notch transit and endure gasoline that costs $5 per gallon, but in fact they don't drive much less than we do. In the United States, automobiles account for about 88 percent of travel. In Europe, the figure is about 78 percent. And Europeans are gaining on us.

The key factor that affects driving habits isn't population density, public transit availability, gasoline taxes or even different attitudes. It's wealth. Europe and the United States are relatively wealthy, but American incomes are 15 to 40 percent higher than those in western Europe. And as nations such as China and India become wealthier, the portion of their populations that drives cars will grow.

2. Public Transit Can Reduce Traffic Congestion

Transit has been on the slide for well more than half a century. Even though spending on public transportation has ballooned to more than seven times its 1960s levels, the percentage of people who use it to get to work fell 63 percent from 1960 to 2000 and now stands at just under 5 percent nationwide. Transit is also decreasing in Europe, down to 16 percent in 2000.

Like auto use, suburbanization is driven by wealth. Workers once left the fields to find better lives in the cities. Today more and more have decided that they can do so in the suburbs. Indeed, commuters are now increasingly likely to travel from one suburb to another or embark upon "reverse" commutes (from the city to the suburbs). Also, most American commuters (52 percent) do not go directly to and from work but stop along the way to pick up kids, drop off dry cleaning, buy a latte or complete some other errand.

We have to be realistic about what transit can accomplish. Suppose we could not only reverse transit's long slide but also triple the size of the nation's transit system and fill it with riders. Transportation guru Anthony Downs of the Brookings Institution notes that this enormous feat would be "extremely costly" and, even if it could be done, would not "notably reduce" rush-hour congestion, primarily because transit would continue to account for only a small percentage of commuting trips.

But public transit still has an important role. Millions of Americans rely on it as a primary means of transportation. Transit agencies should focus on serving those who need transit the most: the poor and the handicapped. They should also seek out the niches where they can be most useful, such as express bus service for commuters and high-volume local routes.

Many officials say we should reconfigure the landscape— pack people in more tightly—to make it fit better with a transit-oriented lifestyle. But that would mean increasing density in existing developments by bulldozing the low-density neighborhoods that countless families call home. Single-family houses, malls and shops would have to make way for a stacked-up style of living that most don't want. And even then the best-case scenario would be replicating New York, where only one in four commuters uses mass transit.

3. We Can Cut Air Pollution Only if We Stop Driving

Polls often show that Americans think that air quality is deteriorating. Yet air is getting much cleaner. We miss it because, while we see more people and more cars, we easily overlook the success of air-quality legislation and new technologies. In April 2004, the Environmental Protection Agency reported that 474 counties in 31 states violated the Clean Air Act. But that doesn't mean that the air is dirtier. The widely publicized failing air-quality grades were a result of the EPA's adoption of tougher standards.

Air quality has been improving for a long time. More stringent regulations and better technology have allowed us to achieve what was previously unthinkable: driving more and getting cleaner. Since 1970, driving—total vehicle miles traveled—has increased 155 percent, and yet the EPA reports a dramatic decrease in every major pollutant it measures. Although driving is increasing by 1 to 3 percent each year, average vehicle emissions are dropping about 10 percent annually. Pollution will wane even more as motorists continue to replace older, dirtier cars with newer, cleaner models.

4. We're Paving over America

How much of the United States is developed? Twenty-five percent? Fifty? Seventy-five? How about 5.4 percent? That's the Census Bureau's figure. And even much of that is not exactly crowded: The bureau says that an area is "developed" when it has 30 or more people per square mile.

But most people do live in developed areas, so it's easy to get the impression that humans have trampled nature. One need only take a cross-country flight and look down, however, to realize that our nation is mostly open space. And there are signs that Mother Nature is gaining ground. After furious tree chopping during America's early years, forests have made a comeback. The U.S. Forest Service notes that the "total area of forests has been fairly stable since about 1920." Agricultural innovations have a lot to do with this. Farmers can raise more on less land.

Yes, American houses are getting bigger. From 1970 to 2000, the average size ballooned from 1,500 square feet to 2,260. But this hardly means we're gobbling up ever more land. U.S. homeowners are using land more efficiently. Between 1970 and 2000, the average lot size shrank from 14,000 square feet to 10,000.

In truth, housing in this country takes up less space than most people realize. If the nation were divided into four-

Left Behind

Left behind in this car culture are central city poor residents without cars, who have become increasingly isolated from the American economy. As Mark Alan Hughes, William Julius Wilson, and other scholars have documented, the steady movement of jobs out of cities and into the suburbs has helped create and sustain the concentrated poverty that is now endemic to America's urban areas. Because new jobs tend to be located in ever-expanding suburbs, which are poorly served by mass transit, poor central city residents find themselves living further and further away from economic opportunities. Evelyn Blumenberg, a professor of urban planning at UCLA [University of California, Los Angeles], found that car-driving residents of the Watts section of Los Angeles have access to an astounding 59 times as many jobs as their neighbors dependent on public transit. Even more isolated are the car-less low-income families that now live in the suburbs—nearly half of all metropolitan poor.

Margy Waller,
"Auto-Mobility: Subsidizing America's Commute?"
Washington Monthly, *October-November 2005.*

person households and each household had an acre, everyone would fit in an area half the size of Texas. The United States is not coming anywhere close to becoming an "Asphalt Nation," to use the title of a book by Jane Holtz Kay.

5. We Can't Deal with Global Warming Unless We Stop Driving

What should be done about global warming? The Kyoto Protocol [an international agreement on climate change] seeks to get the world to agree to burn less fossil fuel and emit less carbon dioxide, and much of that involves driving less. But even disregarding the treaty's economic costs, Kyoto's environmental impact would be slight. Tom M.L. Wigley, chief scientist at the U.S. [National] Center for Atmospheric Research, calculates that even if every nation met its obligation to reduce greenhouse gas, the earth would be only .07 degrees centigrade cooler by 2050.

Wigley favors a much more stringent plan than Kyoto, but such restrictions would severely restrict economic growth, particularly in the developing world. Nations such as China and India were excluded from the Kyoto Protocol; yet if we're serious about reversing global warming by driving less, the developing world will have to be included.

The United Nations' Intergovernmental Panel on Climate Change [IPCC] notes that during the 20th century the earth's temperature rose by 0.6 degrees centigrade and—depending on which of the many climate models turn out to be closest to reality—it expects the temperature to rise 1.4 to 5.8 degrees by 2100.

What does the IPCC think the effects of global warming may be? Flooding may increase. Infectious diseases may spread. Heat-related illness and death may increase. Yet as the IPCC notes repeatedly, the severity of such outcomes is enormously uncertain.

On the other hand, there's great certainty regarding who would be hurt the most: poor people in developing nations, especially those who lack clean, piped water and are thus vulnerable to waterborne disease. The IPCC points out that the quality of housing in those countries is important because simple measures such as adding screens to windows can help prevent diseases (including malaria, dengue and yellow fever) from entering homes. Fragile transportation systems can also frustrate disaster recovery efforts, as medical personnel are often unable to reach people trapped in flooded areas.

Two ways of dealing with global warming emerge. A more stringent version of Kyoto could be crafted to chase the unprecedented goal of trying to cool the atmosphere of the entire planet. Yet if such efforts resulted in lower economic growth, low-income populations in the United States and developing countries would be less able to protect themselves from the ill effects of extreme heat or other kinds of severe weather.

Alternatively, the focus could be on preventing the negative effects—the disease and death—that global warming might bring. Each year malaria kills 1 million to 3 million people, and one-third of the world's population is infected with water- or soil-borne parasitic diseases. It may well be that dealing with global warming by building resilience against its possible effects is more productive—and more realistic—than trying to solve the problem by driving our automobiles less.

> *"Study upon study has been published suggesting that our environment— marked by car-oriented, isolated, un-walkable neighborhoods—is having a deleterious influence on our health."*

Urban Sprawl Resulting from Cars Contributes to Obesity

Carol Lloyd

In the following viewpoint, Carol Lloyd contends that urban sprawl, a product of car dependence, is linked to increasing rates of obesity, high blood pressure, and health problems. Mounting scientific evidence, she proclaims, establishes that people residing in "high-walkability" neighborhoods are leaner and healthier than suburban residents, who walk much less during their commutes and daily activities. While housing developers and transportation policies create even more sprawl and automobile traffic, Lloyd says that smart-growth areas—which are pedestrian, bike, and mass-transit friendly—offer an alternative to crowded city living and isolated, sedentary suburban life. The author is a reporter for the San Francisco Chronicle.

Carol Lloyd, "Where We Live May Be to Blame for Rising Obesity," *San Francisco Chronicle*, April 22, 2007, p. D-2. Republished with permission of *San Francisco Chronicle*, conveyed through Copyright Clearance Center, Inc.

As you read, consider the following questions:

1. According to Lloyd, how did John Holtzclaw's health improve after moving to the city and giving up driving?

2. As stated by Richard Jackson, how has the public reacted to the connection between health and the built environment?

3. How does the author respond to the claim that suburbs are safer and benefit children?

Because he was going to graduate school, retired environmental researcher John Holtzclaw left San Jose and a job that had him driving 25,000 miles a year. His bicycle became his primary form of transportation. After graduation, he settled in an apartment in the Russian Hill-Chinatown area and gave up his car altogether. During those middle years when most of us gain girth, Holtzclaw lost 30 pounds bicycling and walking up the steep hills.

Two years ago [in 2005], Mary Lanosa moved to Pleasant Hill from San Francisco and noticed a change for the worse in her well-being and her weight. Although the length of her commute remained the same, in San Francisco she had used public transportation. "In Pleasant Hill, you have to drive everywhere. Their public transit is lousy," she wrote in an e-mail. "I always felt healthier in the city as I had more opportunities to walk places."

Unhealthy, Unhappy and Fat

We've all heard the tales of urbanites who quit their crime-ridden, inner-city neighborhoods for the safer suburbs. Or affluent retirees who move to bucolic estates in the country. Or working-class and middle-class families who move from one area to another just to find affordable housing or better schools. But moving for health? Isn't health based on genes, diet and the will to use a StairMaster?

Blame your addiction to Häagen-Dazs and your couch-potato personality—and by all means blame your parents. But come on, who ever heard of blaming their muffin tops, love handles and lazy ways on the place they live?

Yet that's precisely the theory posited by a growing body of researchers in public health, urban planning, epidemiology and economics. Ever since two studies linked sprawl and obesity in 2003, study upon study has been published suggesting that our environment—marked by car-oriented, isolated, unwalkable neighborhoods—is having a deleterious influence on our health. In other words, sprawl is making us unhealthy, unhappy and fat.

One early study of 200,000 people, led by urban planner Reid Ewing, found that residents of sprawling communities tended to weigh more, walk less and have higher blood pressure than those living in more densely populated areas. Another study, by health psychologist James Sallis of San Diego State University, concluded that people living in "high-walkability" neighborhoods walk more and were less likely to be obese than residents of low-walkability neighborhoods.

A 2004 study in Atlanta, led by Lawrence Frank, reported that the number of minutes spent in a car could be linked to a risk of obesity. Among the oft-cited conclusions of the study: A typical white male living in an isolated residential-only neighborhood weighs about 10 pounds more than one living in a walkable, mixed-use community.

Ironically, the suburbs were created as protection from the vicissitudes of our older urban environs. In the dense urban areas of the 19th and early 20th centuries, homes sat next to slaughterhouses and tanneries next to cafés.

"Everyone knew someone who had had tuberculosis, and water- and food-borne illnesses were commonplace, so people understood how our environment affected our health," says Richard Jackson, a public health expert who teaches in the

Frank and Ernest used with the permission of the Thaves and the Cartoonist Group.

Department of Environmental Science at UC [University of California] Berkeley and ran the state Department of Public Health under Gov. Arnold Schwarzenegger until 2005.

Jackson says the attempt to create safety and convenience has spawned its own set of problems: "Now we have obesity, diabetes, cancer and joint problems, instead of dysentery. We're richer than before, but things don't feel right. We work harder, we drive farther, we're fatter, we're more depressed. Our lifestyle is making us more unhealthy, and a lot of that is based on our built environment."

In many ways, this line of research makes sense. For decades, growth in American suburbs has outpaced that of city centers—in population and in housing—with average commutes getting longer and the number of walkers and bikers dropping. According to the U.S. Census Bureau, there are 3.5 million "extreme commuters" (people who travel more than three hours a day) in the nation.

An Emerging Field

Researchers say that studies have focused on obesity because it's both so prevalent and so easy to measure. But they add that a sedentary lifestyle (which may or may not manifest in obesity) contributes to many health problems, including asthma, diabetes and high blood pressure.

The idea that America's modern health problems are not all a result of personal lassitude and genetic predisposition but the unintended effects of our built environment hasn't been the easiest concept to sell.

"I talked about the connection between health and our built environment in a speech in 2001," explains Jackson. "It was kind of shocking to people. It was very hard to show the logic sequence—you could argue that poorly designed communities lead to obesity, but there were a lot of steps to show how that was true with research. Now those studies have been done."

And with that momentum, groups like Active Living Research are helping build an interdisciplinary movement that involves health, planning, environmental science and psychology. "This is really a hot topic," says Sallis, who also directs Active Living Research. "It's emerging as a whole field. There are studies going on around the world—and (the National Institutes of Health and the Centers for Disease Control) are both funding research."

Of course, ever since Jane Jacobs declared her love for Greenwich Village in *The Death and Life of Great American Cities* and made it an icon of the new urbanism, planners have been touting the pleasures and practicalities of walkable communities. But, Sallis says, now that it's been picked up by health professionals, the research has more power to change laws and policy. "We're well on the way to provide data to guide designers about policy and how to make walkable communities for all populations."

Still, institutional hurdles remain. Many developers prefer to do as they have always done: build horizontally—an approach that allows them to build in phases and to cut and run if the economy turns sour. Such strategies don't work so well when you're building vertically.

Many transportation engineers also have a stake in maintaining the status quo because funding for transportation has generally been geared toward cars, especially via highways. Since changing road standards and zoning is difficult and time consuming (because these laws tend to be local), as Sallis puts it, our cities' "DNA just keeps replicating itself."

Smart Growth

With a generation raised in sprawl, eating fast food and driving long hours, is it realistic to assume that people's behavior will change if the environment changes? Some studies suggest no—that less-active people will naturally choose communities that allow them to be less active. However, another study showed 30 percent of the respondents reporting that they wanted to live in walkable neighborhoods but were unable to afford them.

So do you have to win the lottery and get an apartment on Russian Hill to experience environmentally induced dieting? Hardly. In fact, some of the Bay Area residents I interviewed discovered that their health improved when they moved out of the city—to what might be characterized as smart-growth hubs.

For instance, Michael Dortch and his wife moved from San Francisco to downtown Santa Rosa. Whereas in the city "almost everything I needed was within two blocks of our apartment . . . (now) my bank and my favorite stores are each at least a half-mile from our home, where I also work." Instead of going to the gym, he takes time out of his workday to go on walks. "I feel better, work is a bit less stressful and I've lost about 25 pounds since we moved," he says. "This may change if I finally, at the age of 51, break down and get my driver's license, but I'm going to try really hard to keep walking anyway."

Margaret Chau and her husband made a similar move, to Millbrae from San Francisco, after carefully researching places that were more walkable and had a pleasant commute. When they lived on the southeast edge of San Francisco near San

Bruno Avenue, the couple felt more isolated. "Plus, we usually had to drive around for 10 to 20 minutes for a parking spot," Chau says, adding that her daily routines are far more pedestrian than they once were.

"I'm now a quarter-mile from all my usual shopping places—Trader Joe's, Peet's and a few other local groceries." Instead of her husband driving through the city to get to Caltrain, he rides his bike along a nature trail for about 11 miles.

Of course, when many families choose a suburban life, they make a clear-eyed choice: to sacrifice the adults' health and well-being (with a longer commute, fewer cultural attractions, etc.) for the children's well-being.

The suburbs are presumably built with children in mind—with crime-free residential neighborhoods, backyards and cul-de-sacs to play in and better schools. But studies have shown that the new suburban realities may be affecting children's health as well.

An estimated 20 percent of school-age children are obese. And only 13 percent of children walk to school, compared with 66 percent in 1973. Sometimes even those playful, active creatures for whom the suburbs were made find themselves stranded like commuters on a long ride to an unhealthy adulthood.

"In recent years, the anti-suburban interests have produced a number of studies that could be called frivolous or even silly, especially in the field of public health."

Urban Sprawl Resulting from Cars Does Not Contribute to Obesity

Wendell Cox

In the following viewpoint, Wendell Cox refutes the body of research that connects obesity to the reliance on automobiles and suburban lifestyles. Cox charges that the methods and data of supporting studies are either skewed or insignificant, failing to establish casual relationships between built environments and physical activity. Moreover, he posits that these analyses fail to include the primary factors of obesity: food consumption and the changing eating habits of Americans. Cox is principal of the Wendell Cox Consultancy in St. Louis, Missouri, and author of War on the Dream: How Anti-Sprawl Policy Threatens the Quality of Life, *from which this viewpoint is excerpted.*

Wendell Cox, "Research Summary: Obesity and Land Use," *Demographia*, August 2009. Adapted from *War on the Dream: How Anti-Sprawl Policy Threatens the Quality of Life*. Lincoln, NE: IUniverse, 2006. Copyright © 2006 by Wendell Cox. All rights reserved. Reproduced by permission of the author.

As you read, consider the following questions:

1. How does the author support his argument that alleged weight differences between suburban and urban residents are unsubstantial?

2. According to Cox, why is the sample in the Atlanta study "representative of nothing"?

3. As stated by the author, how do opponents characterize suburbanization?

In recent years, the anti-suburban interests have produced a number of studies that could be called frivolous or even silly, especially in the field of public health. Obesity has taken center stage, a campaign that seems intent on making sure that how much we eat is kept out of the discussion.

The anti-suburbanites have been trying to demonstrate that obesity has increased in the United States because people who live in suburbs get less physical exercise. The most quoted is a Smart Growth America and Surface Transportation Policy Project report, which used an econometric model to predict a statistically significant relationship between obesity and suburbanization, using a Centers for Disease Control (CDC) data set.

Less than Compelling

However, the report was rife with difficulty. The apparently statistically significant results were insignificant. The statistical method used is highly sensitive to skewing based upon "outliers"—cases far out of the normal range, principally four counties within New York City that are so much more dense than the other observations as to render them unrepresentative. In the face of a general view that obesity is associated with lower incomes, household income data were *excluded* from the analysis, despite being available to the researchers in the CDC data set.

Even so, the results from the questionably designed research were less than compelling. The predicted average weight difference between San Francisco, the nation's least sprawling county outside New York and the most sprawling suburban county was less than 2.5 pounds. The predicted difference between highly urban Cook County (which includes the central city of Chicago) and the most sprawling county in the metropolitan area was less than 1.5 pounds. It is hard to imagine a weight-loss firm purchasing time on late night cable television to tout the potential of its products to trim 2.5 pounds over the course of a lifetime.

Somewhat untypical for what purported to be dispassionate research, members of Congress were briefed and an entire issue of a medical journal (*American Journal of Health Promotion*) was taken over with a summary of the research, along with related articles. Promoters were less than careful as they pointed out that U.S. Centers for Disease Control (CDC) data were used, so that some media outlets referred to the study as a CDC report.

A further installment was provided by Professor Lawrence Frank of the University of British Columbia (UBC), who led researchers on a study of neighborhood obesity in the Atlanta metropolitan area. The results indicated that people who drive more (and live in less urban settings) tend to be more obese. However, the sample included a disproportionate number of people who were in cars more than five hours per day, and can thus be considered representative of nothing. Again, there was a marketing campaign untypical of dispassionate academic research. There were press conferences and an impressive spread in a special *Time* magazine issue on obesity. Again, the study had design flaws. While the researchers managed to collect data on body weight and household income, the survey sought no information on eating habits or diet. Meanwhile, one of the study's coauthors has distanced himself the princi-

A Widespread Prejudice

From Australia to Great Britain (and points in between), there is a drive to use the public purse to expand often underused train systems, downtown condominiums, hotels, convention centers, sports stadia and "star-chitect"-designed art museums, often at the expense of smaller business, single-family neighborhoods and local shopping areas. All this reflects a widespread prejudice endemic at planning departments in universities, within city bureaucracies, and in much of the media. Across a broad spectrum of planning schools and practitioners, suburbs and single-family neighborhoods are linked to everything from obesity, rampant consumerism, environmental degradation, the current energy crisis—and even the predominance of conservative political tendencies.

Joel Kotkin, "The War Against Suburbia,"
Wall Street Journal, *January 14, 2006.*

pal thesis of the marketing campaign, that suburban lifestyles cause obesity: *We do not see it as a causal relationship, necessarily.*

A principal difficulty with the "suburbanization makes you fat" studies is the order of events. The large increase in obesity came after 1980. Yet, there has been little change in urban land-use patterns since 1980. The greatest suburbanization—the major reductions in density—occurred before 1980. A recent study by the Transportation Research Board (TRB), a unit of the National Science Foundation, dismissed the "suburbs make you fat" contentions, stating that "research has not yet identified" sufficient causal relationships to demonstrate that "changes to the built environment would lead to more physical activity."

Other Causes Were Routinely Excluded

However, more fundamentally, studies that exclude plausible causes from their analysis cannot be taken seriously. The econometric researcher has an obligation to include information on every potential contributor to a problem. What might be the most important driver of obesity—food consumption—has routinely been excluded from analyses.

Yet, changing eating habits are a more plausible cause of rising obesity. There are indications that caloric consumption has increased markedly since 1980. One report indicates that there was a more than 15 percent increase in consumption during the first one-half of the 1990s. This idea was rhetorically stated in the title of an article by Dr. Ronald D. Utt of the Heritage Foundation, "Obesity and Life Styles: Is It the Hamburger or Your House?"

Finally, a *Scientific American* review of the obesity literature includes no reference to land use or suburbanization.

The extent to which the anti-suburban claims have degenerated is illustrated by an Ontario College of Family Physicians report, which examined the literature relating to suburbanization and health. The college found, for example, that driving in traffic congestion worsens stress, as it naïvely accepted the fallacious argument that suburbanization increases traffic congestion. They cite research purporting to associate suburbanization with "fear." Other studies associate "roadside blight" or "visual clutter" with suburbanization and make the predictable mental health connections. The array of public health justifications for densification is great indeed, but much more could follow. Perhaps future studies will show causal relationships between suburbanization and bad breath or hemorrhoids—everything "but the kitchen sink."

> "The post-SUV world will come to pass only gradually, but as it does, we can look forward to getting at least some relief from the damage that the reign of the big boxes has done."

Sport Utility Vehicles Harm America

Stan Cox

Stan Cox is a plant breeder and author of Sick Planet: Corporate Food and Medicine. *In the following viewpoint, he declares that crashing sport utility vehicle (SUV) sales is good news. Cox suggests that fewer SUVs on the nation's roads and freeways will result in reduced fuel consumption, fewer automobile fatalities and accidents, and more room to drive. In addition, he states that SUVs offer only slightly more passenger space than smaller vehicles, and the automobile's rugged image runs contrary to its urban use by solitary drivers. The demise of the SUV, however, does not solve the dual problems of depleting oil supplies and rising carbon dioxide emissions, Cox concludes.*

As you read, consider the following questions:

1. How does Cox support his claim that SUVs consume more fuel than the average car?

2. In Cox's view, why do SUVs in particular pose a danger to children?

3. According to Cox, what should be done with unused SUVs?

As peak-oil enthusiasts keep vigil over world petroleum statistics, they can find comfort in America's sudden, rapid descent from a different summit: the peak of sport utility vehicle (SUV) production. In the early 2000s, combined sales of SUVs, pickup trucks, and minivans (which together make up the "light truck" class) caught and surpassed sales of passenger cars. But last week [in July 2008], automakers announced that high gas prices have caused their sales of SUVs and full-size pickups to plummet by as much as 50 percent compared with a year ago. With big-box vehicles waddling off into the sunset, we can expect the nation's roads to become safer and less crowded. But just as the end of the Cold War failed to bring with it a promised peace dividend, the end of the SUV era is unlikely to bring a "green dividend"—unless it is accompanied by much bigger changes. The numbers show that even the complete disappearance of SUVs from the nation's roadways, without other fuel-saving developments, would put only a slight bend in the rising curve of national fuel consumption.

First, the Good News

By 2006, sales of the largest pickup trucks were 2½ times what they had been in 1992; meanwhile, assisted by the so-called "HUMMER tax deduction," sales of 6,000- to 10,000-pound SUVs had risen 25-fold. But as last week's sales figures from Detroit made clear, 2008 will be a very different year. In

May, for the first time in 17 years, the top-selling vehicle model in America was not a pickup truck. In fact, Ford's F-150, the perennial leader, was overtaken by three small import-car models. Ford's June truck sales were down 41 percent from a year ago, and its SUV sales are now in free fall, down 55 percent. Sales of Dodge Ram pickups tumbled 48 percent. General Motors, Ford and Chrysler were hit hard, and all have announced plans to close or suspend production at plants that make trucks and SUVs. The post-SUV world will come to pass only gradually, but as it does, we can look forward to getting at least some relief from the damage that the reign of the big boxes has done: *Less gas will be burned, reducing greenhouse gas emissions*: The average SUV is driven 20 percent more miles per year than is the average car. That, along with its low fuel efficiency, means that it burns more than 800 gallons of fuel per year. The average pickup is only slightly less thirsty, at 700 gallons, compared with just under 500 burned by the average car. But without greater restraint by all drivers, how much can the demise of the SUV reduce fossil fuel consumption? As we will see, not much. *Drivers of all vehicles will be less likely to die in a car crash*: Michael Anderson, assistant professor of economics at the University of California at Berkeley, has done the math showing that increasing popularity of SUVs and pickups led to an increase in annual traffic fatalities. Of the additional deaths, he wrote, "approximately one-fifth accrue to the light trucks' own occupants, and the remaining four-fifths accrue to the occupants of other vehicles and pedestrians." To put it another way, getting most SUVs and pickups off the road will make everyone safer—especially those who don't drive them. In *High and Mighty*, his definitive 2002 book on the SUV, journalist Keith Bradsher described how the taller vehicles block the vision of car drivers and contribute to accidents. Statistics show that a person who's at the wheel of a small, nimble car and appropriately aware of the need to avert danger is much safer than a complacent driver relying solely on the protective bulk of an SUV—a vehicle "designed to overcome its environment, not to respond to it," in the words of writer Malcolm Gladwell. *Fewer children might be run over*: Some, but not all, surveys have shown that, presumably because of poorer visibility to the rear, SUVs and pickups are more likely to be involved in what are called driveway "backover" accidents, most victims of which are children. In one study, backovers were fatal most often when the vehicle was a pickup truck. *There will be more room on the road for everyone—and maybe less road construction*: Small-car drivers know that bottom-of-a-well feeling that comes when you're surrounded on all sides at a traffic light by 3-ton, black-windowed behemoths. Bradsher cites studies demonstrating the various ways in which SUVs clog roadways: that a length of road or street able to accommodate, say, 100 cars can hold only 71 SUVs or 87 pickups; that at busy intersections dominated by SUVs, fewer vehicles can get through a green light before the next change; and that large SUVs sap taxpayers by increasing wear and tear on roads. Indeed, as big-vehicle pressures decline, states and municipalities may be able to give drivers, and the environment, a little break by canceling some of their road-widening plans. *Will we be contending with less road rage?*: A 2004 Canadian study in the journal *Traffic Injury Prevention* found that in "serious" road rage incidents, in which drivers "intentionally damaged or attempted to damage another driver's vehicle, and/or intentionally hurt or attempted to hurt a driver or passenger in another vehicle," SUV drivers were more likely to be perpetrators than were drivers of other vehicle types.

What Will SUV Drivers Drive Next?

Despite being prized for their roominess, most SUVs haul only slightly more people than do cars—on average, not enough riders to fill even the front seat. In advertisements, SUVs are parked on cliff tops, but in real life, 76 percent are

Disproportionate Damage

SUVs [sport utility vehicles] have long come under fire for their height and girth, which can intimidate drivers of smaller vehicles and which also make SUVs three times more likely than cars to roll over. Now safety advocates are taking aim at another SUV trait: their tendency to do disproportionate damage to smaller vehicles. Among crashes in which an SUV strikes a car, there are 16 times as many driver fatalities in the cars as in the SUVs. "The auto industry has paid too little attention to the safety of other motorists," David Pittle of the public-interest group Consumers Union told a Senate panel last week [in February 2003].

Richard J. Newman, "Big, Bad Brutes?"
U.S. News & World Report, *March 2, 2003.*

parked in urban streets, driveways and garages most nights. And despite their hardworking country-and-western image, 60 percent of pickup trucks are owned by urban households and typically ply the streets with empty cargo beds. In a 2005 paper, University of Pennsylvania doctoral candidate Josh Lauer dismissed the SUV's reputation for safety and spaciousness: "Safety is not road safety but personal safety, and space is not interior cargo space but social space, including the ability to traverse the most inhospitable terrain to sequester oneself from the hazards of modern civilization. In this way, the SUV's popularity reflects underlying American attitudes toward crime, random violence, and the importance of defended personal space." Only 13 percent of SUVs are owned by families of 5 or more persons, and a big 40 percent are found in households of only one or two. A report prepared for the U.S. Department of Energy in August 2000 cited a survey of car buyers that found: "The average SUV customer is male, married, aged 45 years, in a household with an income of $94,400. . . . Because SUV owners are fairly affluent, the price of the vehicle and of fuel is not sufficiently important to cause them to consider changing the type of vehicle they drive." But at the time that paper was published, gasoline was at $1.43 per gallon, a price we're certain never to see again. Recent price shocks appear to have changed attitudes even among well-to-do car shoppers, despite the fact that people who can easily afford a $100 dinner check should be unfazed by a $100-plus tank of gas. Without a national survey on the issue, it's hard to predict what will fill the garages of the most affluent drivers in coming years, according to Pamela Danziger. As president of Unity Marketing in Stevens, Penn., a firm specializing in analysis of luxury markets, Danziger predicts that current high-end SUV drivers "will keep them going until their current leases are up or it's time to buy a new vehicle. Then it is likely that they will trade down to a more economical, but no less luxurious vehicle." The well-heeled sport utility driver won't be going extinct. On the day that automakers' dismal June sales figures were announced, Reuters profiled a few members of that species—people like John Stephens:

> Arizona mortgage broker John Stephens uses his big plum-colored Dodge RAM pickup to tow off-road vehicles out to the desert to play. He likes their comfort and space. As he sluiced gallon after gallon of gas at $4.16 a go into his truck at a Scottsdale gas station, Stephens said he was prepared to make certain sacrifices to improve consumption, such as driving more slowly if the government cut speed limits to save fuel. But he would not consider giving up his truck despite getting just 13 miles per gallon. "I'd rather see more drilling and more alternative type fuels, anything to keep the price of gas down," he said.

Possibly the worst news for Detroit in June was that buyers were not just switching models or brands; sales were down

18 percent across the board. With the era of cheap oil over, companies may find that it's hard to build and sell a vehicle that meets both the economic and the psychological demands of drivers. As they scramble to find one, you can bet that they'll want to learn from their previous, ultra-successful SUV market analysis. In his book, Bradsher asks, "Who has been buying SUVs since automakers turned them into family vehicles?" and arrives at this answer:

> They tend to be people who are insecure and vain. They are frequently nervous about their marriages and uncomfortable about parenthood. They often lack confidence in their driving skills. Above all, they are apt to be self-centered and self-absorbed, with little interest in their neighbors or communities. No, that's not a cynic talking—that's the auto industry's own market researchers . . .

But setting up SUV owners as villains is probably not very helpful. (Nor is the SUV's widely discussed appeal to the "reptile brain," an idea hatched by the eccentric French anthropologist Clotaire Rapaille and popularized by Bradsher.) Adapting society to the twin problems of declining oil supplies and rising atmospheric carbon requires that we face an awkward truth: It's not that there are too many SUVs or pickups on the road, it's that too many vehicles of all types are rolling around out there. Many ex-SUV drivers have been trading them in for so-called crossover vehicles (CUVs)—smaller versions of SUVs with car-like unibody construction. But even a mass replacement of SUVs with cars would not make this a fuel-frugal nation. Suppose that all SUV owners in America turned instead to average-efficiency cars or CUVs while retaining current driving habits. That, based on government figures, would reduce fuel consumption by less than 5 billion gallons per year—equivalent to 3 percent of national gasoline consumption. Were all SUVs replaced by those hot-selling Prius hybrids, the switch would save about 7.5 percent. It may be, as two Duke University professors recently recommended, that policy should be focused on replacing the most inefficient vehicles; however, the conservation gains estimated above would not even make up the ground that we lost in the SUV era. Replacing SUVs with standard cars would take us back to the nation's 2003 level of gas consumption; with Priuses, we'd get back to 1999. And much of the good done by those small savings would be canceled out by the deep ecological tire print of the discarded vehicles and the manufacture, sales and eventual disposal of so many new cars. Since 1990, the total number of vehicle-miles traveled in the United States has risen twice as fast as the country's population. Americans appear to be driving less in 2008, but we continue to travel in largely empty vehicles. In 2001 figures for occupancy (the average number of people, including the driver, who ride in each vehicle type) were 1.48 per pickup; 1.57 per passenger car; 1.76 for SUV; and 2.20 for minivan. A North Carolina survey found that over a six-month period in 2001, 78 percent of SUVs on the road had no occupants other than the driver; the figure was the same for pickups and slightly higher than the 76 percent observed for passenger cars. That squares with DOT [Department of Transportation] figures showing that 76 percent of commuter trips are made solo. From the U.S. Department of Transportation (DOT) comes this astonishing comparison: "In 1969, about 20.6 percent of households owned no vehicles [and a minuscule number owned more than three]. By 2001, more households owned four or more vehicles than owned no vehicles." We now have almost 14 million more personal vehicles in the US than we have licensed drivers.

Where Will the SUVs Go Next?

Production of new SUVs and pickups could eventually taper off somewhere near its level of the early 1980s, when sport utility vehicles were used primarily for, well, sport and utility. Meanwhile, a financial system that's still hung over from the pop of the McMansion bubble is sinking even deeper, as— pop!—goes the McMotor bubble. *AutoWeek* reports that "with some 800,000 truck-based sport utility vehicles coming off lease this year, residual values projected three and four years ago will be missed by as much as $6,000 per unit ... Those who lend the money—banks, credit unions, car companies' captive finance arms and others who write leases—will face a tab of nearly $5 billion just in 2008." Abner Perney is a city commissioner in Salina, Kansas, where he owns and runs Abner's Autos, a used car business. He's watching prices of SUVs and pickups sink into a seemingly bottomless pit and expects the lease crunch to trigger "another banking credit mini-crisis" that mirrors the home mortgage fiasco. Perney, who is now running for the Kansas state senate on a low-carbon-emissions platform, adds, "Same thing goes for millions of people who owe much more than their gas hog is worth, when they find themselves in the bind of wanting to sell or having to sell." Many of the oldest, least expensive gas-guzzlers may end up parked with those families who can least afford to feed them. Perney expects used SUVs to move well down the income scale: "Historically, poor folks have big old cars because they depreciate fast, yet they are tough enough to keep on going. Keeping them running is actually cheaper for everything other than fuel and oil, because they're rugged and generally understressed mechanically. The luxury doodads and electronic gizmos are expensive to repair, but you can usually get by without them." If fuel costs keep rising, they could overwhelm those other expenses. Nevertheless, many low-income earners are familiar with having to pay heavy recurring bills because they can't afford big one-time costs up front: Some pay outrageous weekly or daily rents for lousy housing because they can't afford high deposits and advance rent, or are ripped off by check-cashing outfits because they can't put up the minimum deposit for a checking account. Similarly, if the more fuel-efficient vehicles end up with the least affordable price tags on used-car lots, cash-strapped buyers may end up stuck with big, cheap trucks or SUVs. The question of how to keep them running will have to be left for another day.

Taking Back the Streets

In dealing with the aftermath of the SUV boom and bust, some creativity is needed. Maybe a worthwhile complement to the nation's Strategic Petroleum Reserve would be a Strategic Light Truck Reserve. All of those orphaned SUVs and macho pickups could be rounded up, mothballed and designated a public resource. Then over the coming decades, they could be doled out a few at a time to communities, to be shared by all residents for necessary hauling, towing and traveling in larger groups. Because most people need the greater capacity of SUVs and pickups only rarely, such vehicles would seem to be ideal candidates for joint-ownership or sharing arrangements. Tracey Axelsson is executive director of the nonprofit Cooperative Auto Network (CAN) in Vancouver, British Columbia, which is the oldest car-sharing co-op in the English-speaking world. By offering pickup trucks in its fleet, CAN manages to fill members' occasional hauling needs while helping reduce the number of large vehicles on the road. Axelsson hopes "that the old adage is changing—that 'The only thing better than owning a truck is having a friend that does' will become: The only thing better than sharing a truck is spending the money you save from not owning one.'" But, she adds, CAN is part of a coalition of similar groups struggling to develop a general code of ethics for car-sharing. Otherwise, she says, such systems "can fall into the standard drama of providing just another disposable automobile or actually add to the number of cars in a person's toy box." Don Fitz of St. Louis, Mo., who edits the green-social journal *Synthesis/Regeneration* (disclosure: I am on the journal's editorial board) recently laid out a plan for radically reducing the numbers of personal vehicles on the road through combinations of living rearrangements, incentives and disincentives. Some of his recommendations: Cut the workweek to 32 hours or much less, ensure that getting to work is quicker without a car than with one, move jobs closer to residences, and start making it harder to drive by eliminating more parking spaces every year. (The Utah state government recently went to an energy-saving four-day workweek, but without decreasing work hours.) Fitz emphasized, "Increasing trains and buses could be deep green transportation—but if and only if it is part of an actual decrease in the number of automobiles. Likewise, increasing bicycles, scooters, carpooling and car-sharing is truly green transportation only if it is a piece of the big picture of reducing cars." Our vehicle population will eventually shrink, whether it's through choice or necessity. This twilight of the SUV era seems an appropriate occasion to rework our whole concept of personal transportation—and start depopulating America's car dealerships and parking lots.

> "Having an SUV will allow you to be
> prepared for anything."

Sport Utility Vehicles Do Not Harm America

Lee Devlin

In the following viewpoint, Lee Devlin defends the sport utility vehicle (SUV). Despite rising gas prices, Devlin states that SUVs are popular because of their usefulness. From driving through inclement weather to carpooling to hauling heavy-duty cargo, SUVs outperform compact cars, he says. Devlin further suggests that his annual fuel consumption as both an SUV and motorcycle owner is comparable to that of a compact car owner. In fact, he faults critics of SUVs for not recognizing their overall carbon footprints, such as the environmental effects of frequent air travel. The author is an engineering consultant based in Greeley, Colorado.

As you read, consider the following questions:

1. How does Devlin respond to the criticism that most SUV owners do not go off-roading?

2. What is Devlin's view of carbon credits?

Lee Devlin, "In Defense of the SUV," *Devlin Consulting*, December 17, 2008. Reproduced by permission.

3. What recommendations does the author offer SUV owners?

I've written a lot about renewable energy and so people might classify me as an environmentalist, a tree hugger, if you will. I thought it would be time to address the 4700 lb. elephant in the garage. That's right, like many Americans, I own a sport utility vehicle (SUV). It's a 1999 Dodge Durango that I bought 10 years ago [in 1998] and I hope to be able to keep for at least another 10 years.

It seems that over the past few years, SUVs have been getting a black eye in the court of public opinion so I wanted to write a little about why I think they remain so popular in spite of their status as gas guzzlers.

There are those who think that anyone who drives an SUV is an enemy of the environment and deserves to be vilified for it. After all, most commuting is done solo, and it is wasteful to be carrying all the weight of an SUV simply to move a single person around. It's almost as if SUV critics feel everyone should be required to use either public transportation or a compact vehicle that gets at least 40 mpg [miles per gallon]. My Durango gets 14.7 mpg average, 19 mpg highway. In warm weather, I ride a motorcycle which gets about 50 mpg and that helps to improve my annualized personal fuel economy. In the past few years, I've used the motorcycle for nearly half my annual miles driven. A small economy car could provide a similar fuel economy as my combination of SUV/motorcycle, but that solution doesn't work for me. I prefer having an SUV and a motorcycle to having a small economy car.

Fewer Limitations

Why are SUVs still outselling hybrids more than 10:1 and were doing so even when recent U.S. gas prices climbed to over $4/gallon? I'd say that much of the reason is because the SUV has fewer limitations than most other vehicles. They just seem to be able to 'do it all.' For example, there have been several instances where the Durango has allowed me to get home in snowstorms that would have been unthinkable in a 2-wheel drive vehicle. Each time that's happened, the peace of mind that 4WD [four-wheel drive] provided more than paid for its increased operating cost. Many critics of SUVs will point to the fact that SUV owners rarely, if ever, take them off the road. But if you live in any state that gets regular home delivery of snow, you will likely put your SUV in 4WD at least a few times per winter season. For a one-week period around Christmas a few years ago with well above average snowfall, SUVs were the only vehicles with enough ground clearance to make it out of our neighborhood. The Durango also can hold 7 adults, making it possible to leave an extra car in the parking lot when carpooling. I have carried 4' x 8' sheets of plywood in it and filled enough wood to rebuild a deck. I carried the fuselage of my airplane inside it as well as its 300 lb. engine and each of its wings, one at a time, of course. I've towed a camper with it. I've actually driven it off-road along with a 4-person crew to repair a ham radio repeater at the top of a mountain. It's truly a versatile machine with its only limitation being its fuel economy when compared to a compact car.

When I was younger I was a boy scout. The boy scout motto is 'be prepared.' An SUV helps its owner to be prepared for virtually anything. Sure, there are many missions where I could use a more fuel-efficient vehicle, but I don't want to own multiple cars, one for each potential mission. Our garage is only big enough for two cars and a motorcycle. And just owning a vehicle costs money, even if you don't drive it. Each vehicle has a capital expense, which needs to be amortized over the miles driven in its lifetime, along with insurance, ownership taxes, and periodic maintenance. Sitting parked in your garage, a vehicle costs money whether it's used or not. And the capital expense of owning a vehicle usually constitutes a larger per mile expense than its fuel bill.

Vilifying SUV Owners Is a Mistake

Most people who drive an SUV [sport utility vehicle] . . . probably consider themselves to be outdoors people. . . . And outdoors people are often environmentalists. So by vilifying this group, the SUV-haters alienate their own constituents. You may not like driving behind the guy in the Land Cruiser on I-80, but he's probably voting for open space in his community, supporting wilderness bills, and contributing to the Sierra Club. With a little prodding, he might support even more radical environmental measures. . . . But slap a stealth climate change sticker on the bumper, and you've radicalized them. Now they hate "environmentalists" and begin to define themselves as something else.

Auden Schendler,
Getting Green Done: Hard Truths from the Front Lines of
the Sustainability Revolution. *New York: PublicAffairs, 2009.*

My wife has a BMW 328i sedan that gets 28 mpg, about twice the fuel economy of the Durango. It's a great car and a lot of fun to drive. When we go on long trips in nice weather, we often take it instead of the SUV. Recently, we flew to the East Coast for a week and when contemplating which vehicle to leave at the airport, we both independently arrived at the same conclusion. Since it was winter, and we didn't know what kind of weather to expect when we returned, we chose the Durango. Sure enough, when we returned we landed late at night in a blizzard. But it was no problem to get home in the Durango. It would have been a harrowing, white-knuckle, 2-hour drive if we had instead chosen the sedan, and it could have ended up in a ditch in need of a tow, like several others we saw on the way home.

'Fair Share'

The major costs of owning a car can be divided into the categories of purchase price and operating costs. Operating costs are comprised of items such as insurance, taxes, maintenance, and fuel. The annual fuel cost for most vehicles is surprisingly low in comparison to these other costs. Compared to the purchase price, fuel may be just a small percentage per mile. That's why people who can afford to spend $60K on a 10-mpg HUMMER H2 are not deterred by having to spend $5K per year for the fuel. They could instead have a 45-mpg hybrid along with a $1,000 annual fuel bill but it's a not an issue if they can afford the HUMMER's gas. Now I know there are some who think that fossil fuels belong to everyone and it's not fair for someone to use more than their 'fair share.' I have to wonder when a resource is finite and irreplaceable, what would constitute a reasonable 'fair share' per person. Because I use my motorcycle in the warmer months, my SUV has been averaging less than 5,000 miles a year, and so it's actually burning less fuel annually than a compact car racking up 15,000 miles a year. A vehicle's fuel economy isn't the only factor that determines how much of an impact someone is having on the environment. A person's transportation-related carbon footprint also includes the *amount* of travel one does annually.

A Huge Carbon Impact

If your job requires you to travel frequently by jet, you may be using large quantities of fossil fuels even if you don't own a car. I've known people who fly more than 100,000 miles a year and don't seem to realize that it also impacts their overall energy consumption and hence their carbon footprint. I find it particularly ironic when energy efficiency evangelists jet all over the world spreading the gospel about conserving energy as they themselves seem to be unaware that their air travel is generating a huge carbon impact. It's a case of 'do as I say, not as I do.' Sometimes they buy carbon credits, thinking it makes up for their 'unavoidable' energy use. That seems to me as nothing more than purchasing indulgences to assuage their guilt.

Public transportation vehicles use fossil fuels in large quantities, although many public transportation proponents don't seem to realize it. Commercial jets typically average 50 miles per passenger per gallon, buses around 80, and trains around 200. These are typical values, not the maximum theoretical numbers, which would assume 100% seat utilization. Most public transportation vehicles need to have excess capacity and thus travel many miles with empty seats. A person who flies enough to make it to an airline's annual 100K club uses more oil than a HUMMER driver racking up 20,000 miles per year.

Sometimes when people talk about hybrid cars and public transportation, they seem to feel that if everyone would just start using these modes of transportation exclusively, both the fossil fuel depletion and global warming problems would be solved. They won't. Better fuel economy just pushes the problem out a few years since those modes of transportation consume fuel too. And since these more efficient modes are often erroneously considered to be virtually carbon-free, people may be induced to travel more miles annually.

We all like to have our mobility. Our modern society is defined by it. If we had to travel exclusively by foot or on horseback, you can rest assured we'd do a lot less of it. I've certainly done my share of traveling and so I'm in no position to criticize others for their travel habits.

So if you own an SUV, I recommend you keep it. If you feel guilty about it, you can try to drive it fewer miles per year, if possible. You can augment your travel needs with a motorcycle, scooter, or bicycle. Or work from home when you can. Having an SUV will allow you to be prepared for anything and keep you from joining the ranks of those who smugly berate SUVs and their owners with adjectives like 're-volting, insidious, and despicable.'

Periodical Bibliography

The following articles have been selected to supplement the diverse views presented in this chapter.

Allan J. Ashinoff	"Enviro-Liberals Should Love High Oil Prices and Capitalism," *California Chronicle*, November 15, 2005.
Mark Benjamin	"Did I Just Buy an SUV?" *Salon*, January 5, 2009.
Eric Peters	"Unsafe at Any Speed," *American Spectator*, December 10, 2003.
Erin Sherbert	"Fueling the Fire," *Metroactive*, December 12, 2007.
Jeff Siegel	"Why the U.S. Is Not Addicted to Oil," *Treehugger*, June 19, 2008.
Nate Silver	"Nate Silver: The End of Car Culture," *Esquire*, May 6, 2009.
Arthur St. Antoine	"Give Up Your SUV—And Other Nauseating Hypocrisy," Motor Trend Blog, September 2, 2007. http://motortrend.com.
Sam Staley	"Healthy City Living," *Reason*, June 2006.
Margy Waller	"Auto-Mobility: Subsidizing America's Commute?" *Washington Monthly*, October-November 2005.

CHAPTER 2

How Can Driving in America Be Made Safer?

Chapter Preface

As of October 2009, six states—California, Connecticut, New Jersey, New York, Oregon, and Washington—ban drivers from talking on handheld cell phones and require them to use hands-free devices. Twenty-one states prohibit new drivers from all cell phone usage. Eighteen states ban drivers from text messaging. Maine, New Hampshire, and Utah treat cell phone usage by drivers as a distraction issue. For instance, in Utah, it's an offense when the driver on a handheld cell phone commits a moving violation, except for speeding.

Numerous experts report that cell phone–using drivers are as dangerous as drunk drivers. "Epidemiological research has found that cell phone use is associated with a four-fold increase in the odds of getting into an accident—a risk comparable to that of driving with blood alcohol at the legal limit,"[1] states the American Psychological Association. Moreover, a 2009 study by the Virginia Tech Transportation Institute claims that text messaging increases the risk of collision or near collision by 23 percent. The study also found that drivers spent, on average, five seconds eyeing their devices before or near a crash, long enough to travel 100 yards at high speeds.

In July 2009, New York senator Charles Schumer introduced the ALERT Drivers Act of 2009, also known as the Avoiding Life-Endangering and Reckless Texting by Drivers Act. If passed, the law would cut a state's federal highway funding by 25 percent if it does not enforce penalties for texting behind the wheel. Douglas Horn, a trial lawyer and founder of the Horn Law Firm in Missouri, supports the bill: "By withholding substantial federal funds, the ALERT legislation imposes a compelling incentive for states to outlaw texting while driving."[2] On the other hand, Vernon F. Betkey Jr., chairman of the Governors Highway Safety Association, opposes the ALERT Act in its current form: "[T]his is a terrible time to consider reducing highway funding given the economic necessity of these dollars in the states . . . We expect at least 30 more states will act in the next two years—all without federal intervention."[3] The authors in the following chapter investigate how the roads can be made safer for all Americans.

Notes

1. American Pyschological Association, February 1, 2006. www.psychologymatters.org.
2. *BusinessWeek*, September 2009. www.businessweek.com.
3. *BusinessWeek*, September 2009. www.businessweek.com.

| *"Primary enforcement seat belt laws re-
main the best way to raise and maintain high seat belt use rates."*

Primary Seat Belt Enforcement Laws Are Beneficial

Kathryn O'Leary Higgins

Kathryn O'Leary Higgins is a board member of the National Transportation Safety Board (NTSB). In the following viewpoint, O'Leary Higgins endorses the passage of primary enforcement seat belt laws in New Hampshire, the only state without the requirements. She claims that allowing police officers to inspect for and issue citations based on seat belt usage would not only reduce motor vehicle deaths and injuries, but would also help to intercept motorists engaging in at-risk behaviors. Likewise, O'Leary Higgins attributes the failure to use seat belts to costly medical bills and lost wages and productivity, which burden taxpayers and state and federal resources.

Kathyrn O'Leary Higgins, "Testimony of Honorable Kathryn O'Leary Higgins, Board Member, National Transportation Safety Board," The Senate Transportation and Interstate Cooperation Committee, State of New Hampshire On House Bill 383, Primary Enforcement Seat Belt Legislation Concord, NH, April 20, 2009.

As you read, consider the following questions:

1. Why are unbelted vehicle occupants in more danger and more dangerous than belted ones, according to O'Leary Higgins?

2. How does the author address the argument that using seat belts is a personal choice?

3. What are the key provisions of primary seat belt law enforcement, as stated by O'Leary Higgins?

Good morning Chairman [Robert] Letourneau and members of the Committee [Senate Transportation and Interstate Cooperation Committee of New Hampshire]. I am pleased to be here in Concord to testify on behalf of the National Transportation Safety Board regarding primary enforcement seat belt laws.

I want to commend you for considering this measure that will so easily save many motor vehicle occupants from crash-related deaths and injuries.

The National Transportation Safety Board is an independent federal agency charged by Congress to investigate transportation accidents, determine their probable cause, and make recommendations to prevent their recurrence. The recommendations that arise from our investigations and safety studies are our most important product. The Safety Board cannot mandate implementation of these recommendations. However, in our 41-year history, organizations and government bodies have adopted more than 80 percent of our recommendations.

The Safety Board has recognized for many years that motor vehicle crashes are responsible for more deaths than crashes in all other transportation modes combined. Every year, more than 90 percent of all transportation-related deaths are caused by highway crashes. The single greatest defense against highway fatalities is a vehicle's seat belts. When used properly, seat belts reduce the risk of fatal injury to front seat vehicle occupants by 45 percent.

Unfortunately, seat belt use in the United States remains considerably lower than seat belt use in other industrialized nations. Australia and Canada, for example, have use rates well over 90 percent, while seat belt use in the United States is approximately 83 percent. Here in New Hampshire, it is slightly less than 70 percent. New Hampshire is the only state that does not require motor vehicle occupants to use seat belts.

The Safety Board recommended in June 1995 that states enact legislation that provides for primary enforcement of seat belt laws. In 1997, the Safety Board again called for the states to enact primary enforcement and to provide the political will that can enable law enforcement agencies to vigorously enforce this important lifesaving law. The Safety Board maintains a Most Wanted list of safety recommendations because of their potential to save lives. Primary enforcement is one of the issues on that list, the one with the potential to save more lives than any other on the list. It also has the potential to save more lives than probably any other piece of legislation you will consider this year [2009].

Today I want to discuss four elements that support the Safety Board's recommendation on primary enforcement seat belt laws. First, seat belts are effective in reducing motor vehicle injuries and fatalities. Second, the 18 percent of motor vehicle occupants who do not use seat belts engage more frequently in high-risk behavior. Third, the economic cost from the failure to use seat belts is substantial. Finally, primary enforcement seat belt laws do increase seat belt use.

Seat Belts Are Effective

Seat belts are the number one defense against motor vehicle injuries and fatalities. Seat belts restrain vehicle occupants from the extreme forces experienced during motor vehicle crashes. Unbelted vehicle occupants frequently injure other occupants, and unbelted drivers are less likely than belted drivers to be able to control their vehicles. Also, seat belts prevent occupant ejections. Only 1 percent of vehicle occupants using seat belts are ejected, while 30 percent of unrestrained vehicle occupants are ejected. In 2007, 76 percent of passenger vehicle occupants who were totally ejected from a vehicle were killed.

The National Highway Traffic Safety Administration (NHTSA) estimates that from 1975 through 2007, seat belts saved almost 242,000 lives nationwide. According to NHTSA, had all passenger vehicle occupants over age 4 used seat belts in 2007, an additional 5,000 deaths would have been prevented. Unfortunately, some motor vehicle occupants mistakenly believe that they are safer without a seat belt, that their vehicle and/or their air bag provides sufficient occupant protection, or that they will not be in a motor vehicle crash where seat belts would make a difference.

Unrestrained Vehicle Occupants More Frequently Engage in High-Risk Behavior

According to daytime observational surveys, approximately 18 percent of motor vehicle occupants nationwide do not use seat belts. These drivers, who choose not to buckle up, tend to exhibit multiple high-risk behaviors and are more frequently involved in crashes. According to the National Automotive Sampling System (crash data composed of representative, randomly selected cases from police reports), belt use among motorists is lowest in the most severe crashes.

Fatal crashes are the most violent motor vehicle crashes and can result from high-risk behaviors such as speeding and impaired driving. Unfortunately, people who engage in these high-risk behaviors also tend not to use their seat belts. While observational surveys have identified an 83 percent seat belt use rate, use in fatal crashes is significantly lower. From 1998

The Seat Belt Turns 50 Years Old

Over 1 million people wouldn't be with us today if it wasn't for an invention created by a Volvo engineer 50 years ago this week [in August 2009]. The device is the three-point safety belt and the engineer, Nils Bohlin, a man who has not only saved millions of lives, but also reduced the severity of injuries for countless others.

With a background in aeronautical engineering, Bohlin's expertise was in ejecting people from planes, rather than keeping them secured in cars. Using his knowledge of restraints in aircraft, Nils went about creating the three-point safety belt as we know it today.

Kyle Fortune,
"50 Years of Belting Up to Save Lives,"
Irish Times, *August 12, 2009.*

through 2007, more than 820,000 vehicle occupants were involved in fatal crashes. Of those 820,000 occupants, more than 316,000 died. More than 53 percent of the vehicle occupants who died were unrestrained. In New Hampshire, for the same time period, more than 900 vehicle occupants died, and more than 68 percent were unrestrained.

Impaired drivers and teen drivers are also considered high-risk drivers. Seat belt use for these populations is substantially lower than the national observed belt use rate. In 2007, only 27 percent of fatally injured drivers who were violating their state's per se impaired driving statute (had a blood alcohol concentration at or above 0.08 percent) were using seat belts. As for teen drivers, researchers found that while belt use was low in states that authorize primary enforcement (47 percent), it was even lower in states with only secondary enforcement seat belt laws (30 percent).

Economic Costs from the Failure to Use Seat Belts Are Significant

Although opponents to primary enforcement seat belt laws claim that nonuse is a personal choice and affects only the individual, the fact is that motor vehicle injuries and fatalities have a significant societal cost. For example, NHTSA calculated that the lifetime cost to society for each fatality is over $977,000, over 80 percent of which is attributed to lost workplace and household productivity. In 2007, more than 5,000 lives and billions of dollars might have been saved if everyone had used a seat belt.

NHTSA estimates that each critically injured survivor of a motor vehicle crash costs an average of $1.1 million. Medical expenses and lost productivity account for 84 percent of the cost of the most serious level of non-fatal injury. In a 1996 study, NHTSA found that the average inpatient cost for unbelted crash victims was 55 percent higher than for belted crash victims. In 2000 alone, seat belts might have prevented more than 142,000 injuries.

While the affected individual covers some of these costs, those not directly involved in crashes pay for nearly three-quarters of all crash costs, primarily through insurance premiums, taxes, and travel delay. In 2000, those not directly involved in crashes paid an estimated $170 billion for crashes the occurred that year; $21 billion, or 9 percent of total economic costs, were borne by public sources (federal and state government). Motor vehicle injuries and deaths experienced by unbelted vehicle occupants cost the nation's taxpayers an estimated $26 billion just for medical care, lost productivity, and other injury related costs.

The emotional and financial costs to New Hampshire are just as staggering. In 2007, 76 vehicle occupants (age 18 and older) died; more than 70 percent were not using the available seat belts. NHTSA estimates that if everyone in New Hampshire used a seat belt, New Hampshire would prevent an additional 20 fatalities and more than 750 injuries, saving the state's taxpayers more than $85 million. In 2000, the most recent year for which data is available, the total economic cost of motor vehicle crashes that occurred in New Hampshire was more than $1 billion.

Primary Enforcement Seat Belt Laws Do Increase Seat Belt Use

Primary enforcement seat belt laws remain the best way to raise and maintain high seat belt use rates. With primary enforcement, police officers are authorized to execute a traffic stop and cite unbelted vehicle occupants without needing another reason for making the stop. According to the National Occupant Protection Use Survey (September 2008), seat belt use in primary enforcement law states was 88 percent, while the belt use rate in secondary enforcement law states was only 75 percent. States that recently enacted primary enforcement seat belt laws have experienced increased seat belt use rates ranging from almost 5 to almost 18 percentage points. The increased use is based on the perceived risk of being stopped.

Support for Primary Enforcement

American citizens support primary enforcement. NHTSA conducted a survey in 2003 to determine the public's opinion on primary enforcement seat belt laws. Overall, 64 percent of the population surveyed supported primary enforcement. Among people from states with secondary enforcement seat belt laws, more than half (56 percent) approved of primary enforcement. Minority populations are strong proponents of primary enforcement. For example, 74 percent of Hispanics surveyed and 67 percent of African Americans surveyed endorsed primary enforcement, as opposed to 62 percent of whites. Traffic crashes affect people of all ethnic backgrounds.

Key provisions of a comprehensive primary enforcement seat belt law should include coverage of all vehicle occupants in all seating positions, coverage of all vehicles, and sufficient penalties to promote compliance with the law. By allowing police officers to stop vehicles directly for seat belt violations, New Hampshire shows that it takes seat belt use very seriously.

The Safety Board believes that House Bill 383 will save lives and reduce injuries. Enacting this bill is likely the most important lifesaving, injury mitigation, and health care cost reduction measure you can take this session. It costs nothing, but will save much. [The bill was not passed.]

"Failure to wear a seat belt does not cause accidents, nor does it prevent one."

Seat Belt Laws Are Intrusive

Brian Tilton

New Hampshire does not have a primary seat belt enforcement law, wherein motorists and passengers can be stopped and ticketed solely for not buckling up. In the following viewpoint, Brian Tilton opposes such laws on several grounds. He insists that they result in unfair arrests, opening the door to unwarranted searches, seizures, and other civil liberties violations. Seat belts are not always effective, Tilton adds, and have even contributed to serious injuries and deaths. Wearing a seat belt is ultimately a personal choice best increased through education, not government coercion, the author contends. Tilton is the host of Bulldog Live!, *a radio show based in Bow, New Hampshire.*

As you read, consider the following questions:

1. What argument does the author present against drivers wearing seat belts?

Brian Tilton, "Testimony to Senate Transportation Committee," The Senate Transportation and Interstate Cooperation Committee, State of New Hampshire On House Bill 383, Primary Enforcement Seat Belt Legislation Concord, NH, April 20, 2009. Reproduced by permission of the author.

2. How does the author reply to the proposition that primary enforcement seat belt laws reduce insurance rates?

3. What research does Tilton present to back his position that seat belts may not save lives?

NH [New Hampshire] is unique in a lot of ways. There's a lot of things we have, and there's a lot of things we don't have, and that's not a bad thing. NH doesn't require seat belt use for adults, and yet, we have one of the lowest highway fatality rates in the country per miles driven.

Expanding Police Powers

One of the main problems I have about a primary seat belt law is the concern for civil liberties. Last April [in 2008], I was reading a news story online from a television station [in] Hagerstown, Maryland, reporting on their "Click It or Ticket" campaign. In the story, they interviewed Sergeant Chris Sasse of Maryland State Police who said, after making a number of points to buckle up, "Don't make me come lock you up." I was shocked by that, and I questioned the reporter in that story why the trooper wasn't challenged on that remark. I received no response.

Just a week ago [in April 2009], I learned that in 2001 the U.S. Supreme Court ruled in *Atwater v. City of Lago Vista* that police can arrest you for not wearing a seat belt. The case involves a woman who [was] not buckled up, and neither were her children. The maximum fine was $50.00. Upon learning this, I did some further investigating. I found out that many other states are arresting people for not wearing seat belts:

• Indiana State Police conducted a blitz just before St. Patrick's Day. There were 267 arrests, 33 of them for not wearing a seat belt.

- Connecticut State Police reported making 148 arrests for seat belt violations in 4 days during the 2008 Christmas season.

- In response to the *Atwater* case, Oklahoma lawmakers had to respond to the concerns of arrests for seat belt violations.

- A 20-year-old man from New York was fighting a seat belt ticket he received, but the court system lost his case and his license got revoked, and he was arrested and had to spend time in central booking with murderers, rapists and armed robbers awaiting his processing.

Once a person has been arrested for a violation whose punishment is only a fine, it opens the door for police to engage searches and seizures of property.

Your vehicle can be stopped anytime, day or night, by the police merely under suspicion a seat belt is not being used. And even if mistaken, once the vehicle is stopped, the officer can begin routine interrogation and testing—force occupants to exit—visually check out the contents of the inside of the vehicle looking for any kind of a violation of the law, all without the right of legal counsel; all under the pretense of not using a seat belt. Even with a medical exemption.

Under this law, a seat belt violation fine will be issued against the driver even if the driver is using a seat belt but a passenger is not, and even if the driver did not know about it. Drivers, therefore, could easily become distracted while driving by a constant watch of passengers, both adults and children in the rear seat.

Driver Behavior

The act of wearing a seat belt does not prevent accidents. Speeding, texting, changing lanes without looking or using a turn signal, eating, reading, tailgating, failure to yield, run[ning] stop signs/red lights—they all cause accidents! Failure to wear a seat belt does not cause accidents, nor does it prevent one.

If anything, an argument can be made that people who wear seat belts are more prone to speeding and tailgating because they have a certain invincibility factor strapped to them.

Playing with Lives

My brother was in a car accident in Connecticut, which has a primary enforcement law. He doesn't like seat belts, but he follows the law. One day he was T-boned by a speeding and unlicensed driver. His seat belt failed to operate. He got knocked across the car, which saved his life. He was threatened with a ticket for not wearing a seat belt. The officer concluded that he lived because he was not buckled up and was not given a ticket. He feels it should be his personal choice. The law almost killed my brother.

My sister suffered a severe injury in a crash from her seat belt. She doesn't want to wear it, but her state pulls her over now for simply not wearing it.

A friend of mine on the other hand survived a 50 mph [miles per hour] crash when someone pulled out in front of him because he was wearing his seat belt. But my friend would always wear a seat belt—he doesn't need a law to tell him to.

Myself, I wear it because I want to. My father taught me to. My father recently died; I don't need the government to take his place.

Lower Insurance Rates

One of the claims of proponents of a seat belt law is that passing a mandatory law will save lives and lower insurance rates. Please keep in mind that New Hampshire drivers have some of the lowest insurance rates in the country. I lived in a state (Maryland) that had the highest seat belt compliance rate, 93%. My insurance premiums were more than double there.

Right to Refuse

A person has the right to refuse any health care recommendation. No non-psychiatric doctor would dare attempt to force a person to use a medical device or take a drug or have surgery or other medical treatment without full consent. Yet politicians force motorists to use a health care device, a seat belt, against their will under threat of punishment that could include jail.

The hundreds of millions of dollars spent in support of seat belt laws have been wasted. Not one penny of that money has ever prevented even a single traffic accident, the real cause of highway fatalities. We don't need millions of dollars for stricter seat belt law enforcement. Instead, we need more responsibly educated drivers, safer vehicles, and better roads to prevent traffic accidents.

William J. Holdorf, "The Fraud of Seat Belt Laws,"
Freeman, vol. 52, no. 9, September 2002.

New Jersey was one of the first states to pass a seat belt law. They have the highest insurance rates in the country. Connecticut also has a primary seat belt law, they have the second or third highest insurance rates in the country.

Besides, many insurance companies already make you promise to wear a seat belt and some may even refuse coverage for injuries sustained for failing to wear one. And lastly, the medical coverages are very limited on most policies, so I would argue that any benefit from lower insurance premiums if all the other so-called benefits of such a law would be negligible.

I'm also afraid that dictating behavior to lower an insurance or societal cost will lead to other laws regulating behavior because it might cost money. Eating too much, skydiving, boating on rivers, lakes and oceans carry their share of risks, too. Dictating other people's behavior because of what it might cost is not freedom, that's socialism.

Federal Money

NH stands to gain $3.7 million in federal funds (my money, which is being borrowed from China that we may never be able to repay). Beware, there will be a lot of strings attached. Some states have actually lost money for not having tough enough seat belt laws, not giving out enough tickets or not conducting enough "Click It or Ticket" campaigns.

- Last month, the state of Kansas, which has a higher seat belt usage percentage than NH, was told that it will lose out on a federal grant of $11 million plus $500,000 per year if it doesn't pass tougher laws.

- Last year, Florida was told if it didn't pass a tougher seat belt law, it would not receive $35 million in federal funds, plus it was given a deadline to do it. They refused.

You always see news stories of people who die in auto accidents and they were not wearing a seat belt. Do you ever see news stories of people who died in car crashed and were wearing a seat belt? What about injuries caused by seat belts? The problem is seat belt usage is not 100% effective. It's a huge chance every time you take to the road. What I resent is the state making that life or death decision for me.

Usage Statistics

Last time this bill was debated two years ago, the members of this committee and the full senate held the belief that seat belt usage is a matter of personal choice and that education is the best way to increase usage. I believe none of that has changed. If you voted in favor of personal freedom last time, please maintain that position. I understand there is pressure to get federal money because of the economic times. But from 2007 to 2008, NH's seat belt usage went up 5 percentage points, even surpassing states with mandatory laws. The national average of seat belt usage went up only 1%. Education works. Nagging by children works. The dinging in the car works. New Hampshire has made tremendous strides in voluntary seat belt usage. It's hard to do better. Common sense is not dead. Let's keep it the New Hampshire Way and prevent creating new police powers that will not only endanger police officers lives as they would be turned into roving ATM machines for government to keep the federal money flowing, but also create more distrust of government when the handcuffs appear for a violation payable by a fine.

While seat belt law supporters want the public to believe that passing a primary enforcement law will reduce highway fatalities, the government's own 1998 report documented just the opposite. In the federal publication "Traffic Safety Facts 1998," under the heading "Occupant Protection," is the following information:

> "A 1995 NHTSA [National Highway Traffic Safety Administration] study, *Safety Belts Use Laws: An Evaluation of Primary Enforcement and Other Provisions*, indicates that states with primary enforcement safety belt laws achieved significantly higher belt use than did those with secondary enforcement laws. The analysis suggests that belt use among fatality injured occupants was at least 15 percent higher in states with primary enforcement laws."

In other words, while primary enforcement does increase forced seat belt use, there is also a 15 percent increase in fatalities as compared with states with secondary enforcement laws. That is, the very purpose of forcing seat belt use is defeated by an increase in highway fatalities in states with primary enforcement laws, according to this study.

> "If [underage drinking] laws are en-
> forced to the extent possible, further re-
> ductions in youthful deaths and inju-
> ries could be realized."

Some Underage Drinking and Driving Laws Reduce Fatal Crashes

ScienceDaily

ScienceDaily asserts in the following viewpoint that numerous laws aimed at reducing underage drunken driving are effective. According to ScienceDaily, a major study demonstrates that four of six policies decrease fatalities and injuries caused by drinking and driving minors: possession of alcohol, purchase of alcohol, driver's license sanctions, and zero tolerance for alcohol consumption and driving. The study also found, ScienceDaily claims, that general laws also reduced fatal crashes, including blood alcohol concentration (BAC) limits for motorists and seat belt usage requirements. ScienceDaily is a science and research news Web site.

"Some Underage Drinking Laws Reduce Drinking-and-Driving Fatal Crashes Better than Others," *ScienceDaily*, April 7, 2009. Reproduced by permission.

As you read, consider the following questions:

1. As stated by James C. Fell, why did the number of fatal car crashes involving drunken minors fall between 1982 and 2004?

2. What other general driving laws, according to Science-Daily, are effective against drunk driving?

3. What are the study's implications for policy makers, in Alexander C. Wagenaar's view?

Although US laws pertaining to a minimum legal drinking age (MLDA) changed many times during the 1970s and 80s, currently all states require a minimum legal age of 21 for both the purchase and public possession of alcohol. While additional MLDA laws exist, not all states have adopted them, and their strength and enforcement appear to be quite variable.

A new study has identified four underage drinking laws that lead to reductions in underage drinking-and-driving fatal crashes: possession, purchase, use and lose, and zero tolerance.

"Most people think that each state has only one underage drinking law, that it is illegal to drink alcohol in public if you are younger than age 21," said James C. Fell, senior program director at the Pacific Institute for Research and Evaluation and corresponding author of the study. "In fact, there are at least two core underage drinking laws that each state has: possession and purchase. We also discovered in our research at least 16 laws pertaining to underage drinking, or to underage drinking and driving. Between 1982 and 2004, there was a 62 percent decrease in drinking drivers under age 21 involved in fatal crashes compared to a 33 percent decrease in drinking drivers aged 21 or older in fatal crashes. Certainly part of this difference was due to raising the MLDA to 21 during that time period."

Adding to the problem of underage drinking and driving, noted Alexander C. Wagenaar, Ph.D., a professor of epidemi-

"Teen drunk drivers," Cartoon by Ed Fischer. www.CartoonStock.com.

ology in the College of Medicine at the University of Florida, is that the US has relatively early licensure of young drivers ... typically 16 in the US compared to 18 in most other developed countries.

"Most youth in the US have easy access to an automobile," said Wagenaar, "along with very limited options in terms of mass transit. The result is common use of cars by teenagers, which contributes to the crash problem since teens have much higher crash rates per mile driven than the general adult population of drivers."

Four of Six

For this study, Fell and his colleagues analyzed data covering a 23-year period from 1982 through to 2004, using the Alcohol

Policy Information System (1998–2005), the Digest of State Alcohol-Highway Safety Related Legislation (1983–2006), the Westlaw database, and the Fatality Analysis Reporting System data set (1982–2004). Study authors selected six underage drinking laws for analysis because they could obtain dates when they became effective in each state. Four general impaired-driving and traffic safety laws were also included because there is substantial evidence of their effectiveness with drivers of all ages.

"We found that four of the six underage drinking laws that we examined were effective in reducing the rate of drinking drivers aged 20 and younger in fatal crashes," said Fell, "while controlling for many other factors that could have accounted for the decrease. Collectively, these four laws—possession, purchase, use and lose, and zero tolerance—save an estimated 864 lives each year."

Fell said these findings confirm earlier research, while using a stronger design. "Our analysis shows that raising the drinking age to 21 in all states was, and continues to be, a very effective measure," he observed. The study also found that three of the four more general laws that target all drivers were clearly effective: 0.08% blood alcohol concentration [BAC] illegal per se law, secondary or upgrade to a primary safety belt law, and an administrative license revocation law.

"We can see that both adults and teens are affected by .08 BAC limits for driving, administrative license suspension laws for driving under the influence of alcohol, and laws requiring safety belt use," said Wagenaar. "All three of those policies significantly reduced car crash deaths."

"These findings point to the importance of both key underage drinking laws and traffic safety laws in efforts to reduce underage drinking drivers in fatal crashes," said Fell. "If these laws are enforced to the extent possible, further reductions in youthful deaths and injuries could be realized. For example, the 15 states that do not have Use and Lose laws—

where there is a driver's license sanction for an underage drinking violation—should seriously consider adopting them. Use and Lose laws were associated with a significant 5 percent decrease in the rate of underage drinking drivers in fatal crashes, and are currently saving an estimated 132 lives each year in the 35 states and the District of Columbia that have these laws."

Wagenaar said these findings have clear implications for policy makers. "These comprehensive analyses using the latest data confirm effective steps to reduce deaths due to car crashes: a legal drinking age of 21; lower allowable blood-alcohol limits for drivers; strong laws requiring safety belt use; and immediate administrative driver's license suspension of anyone caught driving with a blood/breath alcohol level over the legal limit. These laws have already saved thousands of lives per year in the US, and could save even more lives if all states fully implemented them."

Co-authors of the ACER paper were Deborah A. Fisher, Robert B. Voas, Kenneth Blackman, and A. Scott Tippetts, all of the Pacific Institute for Research and Evaluation. The study was funded by the National Institute on Alcohol Abuse and Alcoholism, and the Robert Wood Johnson Foundation.

| "For all the efforts aimed at educating kids about the dangers of drinking and driving, and all the laws cracking down on the sale of alcohol to minors, the statistics remain alarming."

The Effectiveness of Underage Drinking and Driving Laws Is Uncertain

Ryan Blitstein

In the following viewpoint, Ryan Blitstein writes that laws targeting underage drinking and driving are not wholly effective. Blitstein acknowledges that zero-tolerance alcohol mandates have reduced some figures, but alleges that other trends are discouraging. For example, he argues that research has shown that minors' drinking habits failed to change in some states and large percentages of college students still reported bingeing on alcohol and driving after heavy drinking. The most effectual underage drinking and driving policies are comprehensive, according to Blitstein. The author is a Chicago-based journalist and contributing editor at Miller-McCune, *an academic research magazine.*

As you read, consider the following questions:

1. What did a 2004 study reveal about underage drunken driving by males in states with zero-tolerance laws, as stated by Blitstein?

2. What is a significant concern about underage drinking laws, in Blitstein's view?

3. How can alcohol regulation have an "economic bent," according to the author?

Decades of studies have proven a link between alcohol and the traffic crashes that lead to thousands of deaths every year, particularly among youths. Politicians have shown a renewed interest recently in doing something about it: In 2006, a congressional bill authorized $18 million in new federal funds to combat underage drinking, including a national media campaign, money for community-based prevention groups and scientific research. Last March [2008], the acting U.S. surgeon general launched a "Call to Action on Underage Drinking" with similar designs. Yet for all the efforts aimed at educating kids about the dangers of drinking and driving, and all the laws cracking down on the sale of alcohol to minors, the statistics remain alarming.

In 2005, for example, 3,467 drivers between the ages of 15 and 20 were killed, according to the U.S. Department of Transportation. More than a quarter had been drinking alcohol. Of 159 million alcohol-impaired driving trips in the United States in 2002, more than 10 percent were made by 18- to 20-year-olds. And those younger drivers were more likely to end up in crashes than more mature counterparts.

Nevertheless, many of these figures have decreased during the past several years, at least partly due to zero-tolerance drunken driving laws—suspending the licenses of young adults caught driving with any amount of alcohol in their blood. Whereas the legal limit for drivers over 21 may be 0.08–0.10

percent blood alcohol content (BAC), these rules make it illegal for those under 21 to drive with BAC of 0.02 or more—even a single beer would put many above that limit. All 50 states have now enacted these rules, spurred by a 1995 federal law mandating the government to withhold highway aid funding for states that failed to pass them. Several set the limit even lower, at 0.00 percent.

Mixed Results

Since then, several research teams have shown that the laws decreased alcohol-related traffic deaths, but they've had mixed results in analyzing that change. A 2001 paper found a drop in the frequency of driving after drinking in states where the rules went into effect, but no change in the amount of underage drinking. Three years later, another study produced opposite results: Underage males reduced heavy drinking in zero-tolerance states but drove after drinking at rates similar to the control group. At least one researcher suggested that any effect from the zero-tolerance laws could be explained by broad changes in societal norms, such as the idea of using designated drivers, along with other anti-alcohol regulations and initiatives.

Lan Liang, then an economics professor at the University of Illinois–Chicago, and Jidong Huang, then a graduate student at the school, decided to take a crack at explaining the effects. (Liang is now at the government's Agency for Healthcare Research and Quality, and Huang is with NERA Economic Consulting.) They used one of the largest data sets of people aged 18 to 21, the Harvard School of Public Health College Alcohol Study, which covers 14,000 students at 120 colleges in 40 states. As in similar analyses, the control group was students who turned 21 and wouldn't be affected by zero-tolerance laws.

The overall results were discouraging: Two-thirds of the students said they had a drink in the previous 30 days, half

Harsh Penalties Are Ineffective

Simply passing stricter underage drinking laws, with harsh penalties for parents and children, is ineffective. This approach does little to counter the current startling trend of alcohol abuse by minors. The current rash of underage drinking came about after a decade when lawmakers raised the drinking age and increased enforcement. Glamorization of alcohol and drinking is furthered and reinforced by media hype surrounding passage of these laws.

Bryan Knowles,
"Can Tougher Laws Slow Underage Drinking?"
SpeakOut.com, January 9, 2001.

said they engaged in binge drinking (five drinks for males, four for females) in the past two weeks. Forty percent had recently driven after drinking, 20 percent after binge drinking.

"It's pretty striking how many people do what we consider to be pretty dangerous things, but this data correlates with other studies pretty well," Liang said.

When they looked at where students were doing their drinking, though, the researchers discovered a more auspicious trend. In states where zero-tolerance laws went into effect, underage drinkers who drank away from their homes were about 26 percent less likely to drive after drinking. The data also suggested small decreases in the amount of binge drinking in general and drinking away from home, though these weren't as significant.

"It's an ingenious analysis," said Henry Wechsler, director of the Harvard study that provided the raw data. "It's hard to attribute change to a single law, but in this case, they seem to have done it."

Behind Closed Doors

While a drop in drunken driving is good, the dynamic Liang describes could pose other problems. A significant, activist minority is concerned that underage drinking laws already push alcohol behind closed doors, into places with less adult supervision and regulation.

They "have removed consumption from bars and large public venues and moved it to dark corners and off-campus locations," said John McCardell, the former Middlebury College president, now director of Choose Responsibility, an organization that advocates lowering the drinking age to 18 and creating an "alcohol license" for those under 21. By encouraging young drinkers not to drive, zero tolerance might exacerbate these problems.

Some researchers, and many state legislators, support alcohol regulations with a more economic bent, such as restrictions on "happy hour" drink specials in college towns—higher prices often decrease drinking. Others, including McCardell, favor education programs that take a realistic approach, emphasizing harm reduction instead of "temperance lectures."

Most studies have shown that the more comprehensive the laws and programs, the lower the incidence of underage drinking and driving. Despite disagreements over specifics, it's clear to researchers that parents and other private citizens can't tackle underage drinking and driving alone.

"They can't just turn to society and say, 'It's up to you to control students,'" Wechsler said. "States have to deal with this problem, and local municipalities have to deal with it, too."

> *"Four years after Wisconsin adopted a graduated driver's license law, accidents among teenage drivers are at their lowest point in a decade."*

Graduated Driver's Licenses Reduce Youth Accident Rates

Stacy Forster

In the following viewpoint, Stacy Forster writes that since Wisconsin enforced a graduated driver's license law in 2000, the roads have been safer. The law restricts the number of passengers and times of day a newly licensed teen can drive for nine months, Forster states, and, as a result, the annual percentages of accidents and fatal crashes involving adolescent drivers have dropped greatly. She adds that both parents and teens agree that it allows inexperienced drivers to gain experience behind the wheel with fewer distractions and risks, but that not all young people comply. Forster is a reporter for the Milwaukee Journal Sentinel.

As you read, consider the following questions:

1. How does Forster describe teen drivers before the graduated licensing law went into effect in Wisconsin?

Stacey Forster, "Crashes Among Teen Drivers at 10-year Low: Drop Credited to State's Graduated License Law," *Milwaukee Journal Sentinel*, July 12, 2006, p. B1. Copyright © 2006 by Milwaukee Journal Sentinel. Republished with permission of *Milwaukee Journal Sentinel*, conveyed through Copyright Clearance Center, Inc.

2. How does Maureen Smith view the restriction on the number of occupants she can drive?

3. According to Luther Olsen, why do parents appreciate the graduated licensing law?

Four years after Wisconsin adopted a graduated driver's license law, accidents among teenage drivers are at their lowest point in a decade, according to a *Journal Sentinel* analysis of state Department of Transportation figures.

Julie Shiff, mother of a 16-year-old new driver, is a believer in the law especially after her son's recent ride home from a Milwaukee concert with friends.

Dillon Shiff and a couple of buddies were being driven by a friend who had recently graduated out of state restrictions on such things as the number of passengers allowed in the car with a new driver. The group was distracted trying to find the right route home, and the friend got into a minor accident.

"They're not driving fast, they're just talking and listening to music and being kids," said Julie Shiff, of Grafton. "This was their gimme, their one chance to wake up and understand that you're not infallible, that you have to take being behind the wheel seriously."

The First Nine Months

Gone are the days when turning 16 meant squealing out of the school parking lot with a carload of friends. Now, to improve safety and to reduce accidents, the newest drivers must operate with restrictions on the number of passengers in the car and the hours they're allowed behind the wheel. The restrictions are in place for the first nine months that a teen has a license.

"Accidents are continuing to drop, which is what we all want," said Sen. Luther Olsen (R-Ripon), who led the push for the graduated license law, which fully took effect in 2000.

"Anything we can do to further the drop is a step in the right direction without taking too many rights away from new drivers."

In Wisconsin, 28,592 drivers between the ages of 16 and 19 were involved in motor vehicle crashes in 2004, the latest year for which figures are available. That's the lowest total since at least 1994.

Fewer teens were involved in accidents in 2004 even though more of them were on the road than a decade earlier. In 1994, 15.7% of all teenage drivers were involved in a crash; in 2004, it was 12.7%.

In the four years before the graduated license went into effect, an average of nearly 32,000 teenage drivers were involved in accidents each year. The annual average in the four years since the law went into effect was 29,715, a 7% drop. When it comes to the most serious accidents those in which someone was killed or injured the annual average dropped nearly 12%. The reduction in accidents is even greater among 16-year-old drivers, who are subject to the graduated license restrictions.

The average annual number of 16-year-olds involved in all accidents is down 17% in four years after the law took effect compared with the four years before the law began. And the number of 16-year-old drivers involved in fatal or injury crashes dropped even more—22%.

A national study of graduated driver's license programs was released this month [July 2006] by Johns Hopkins Bloomberg School of Public Health's Center for Injury Research and Policy and the Johns Hopkins School of Medicine. It shows that the programs reduced the incidence of fatal crashes involving 16-year-old drivers by an average of 11%.

The study shows that in the states with the most comprehensive programs which includes Wisconsin there was a 20% reduction in fatal crashes involving 16-year-old drivers.

While that study did not have specific figures available for Wisconsin, the *Journal Sentinel*'s separate analysis shows the average number of 16-year-olds involved in fatal accidents dropped 18.5% after the law went into place.

Do Teens Follow the Law?

Because of the law, new drivers such as Maureen Smith take to the roads in smaller steps.

She's looking forward to driving with her friends in the car, but Smith, a 16-year-old who attends Wauwatosa East High School, said she appreciates having time to become comfortable with driving before facing greater distractions.

"I don't think I'd be able to drive with a lot of people in the car at this point in my driving life," she said. "I'm not sure how fun it would be for a new driver to have people in the back yelling at each other."

Smith's 17-year-old brother, Patrick Smith, recently had the requirements lifted from his license. He said he, too, understood the principle behind them, but he and Maureen agreed that they don't think many teens comply.

"I find it necessary in theory, but in practice I don't, because people don't follow it," Patrick Smith said, adding that "it does make for safer driving and it's less distracting."

Olsen, the state lawmaker, said parents appreciate the law because it gives them firm limits to enforce on their children's driving.

Julie Shiff said her son's friend's accident has prompted her and her husband to insist that Dillon follow the rules even after the nine-month period expires.

"I'm sure there will be times when he fights it . . . but I don't care if they have to follow each other in six cars," Julie Shiff said.

Dillon Shiff, who got his license in June, said he understands such limits might be necessary when he's new to driving but expects his confidence in driving alone to grow quickly.

"If I get a ticket or get in a crash, I understand it, but if nothing's happened, I should get some more responsibility," he said.

Enhancements could be made to the limits, Olsen said. He would like the state to restrict new drivers from using cell phones. A bill sponsored by Olsen and Rep. Jerry Petrowski (R-Marathon) passed easily in the state assembly during the 2005–'06 legislative session but didn't advance in the senate.

Olsen said he was recently in the passenger seat with his son, who received his license two months ago, when his son's cell phone rang.

"He had to get on the phone, and all of a sudden we were on the gravel," Olsen said.

> "State officials, traffic safety advocates and even teenagers acknowledge that many flout the [graduated licensing] law."

Graduated Driver's Licenses May Not Reduce Youth Accident Rates

Tom Davis

Tom Davis is an award-winning journalist and was a mental heath columnist for the Record *in Bergen County, New Jersey. In the following viewpoint, the author argues that New Jersey's graduated driver's licensing law has failed to safeguard young drivers and passengers. He alleges that parents, police, and state officials are questioning whether the policy—which restricts the hours and number of passengers allowed for a new driver—has contributed to a spike in fatal crashes involving teens. Among the concerns, Davis reiterates, are the elimination of free behind-the-wheel driver education programs, the lack of parental supervision and guidance, and the lax treatment of graduated driver's licensing violations by overburdened state agencies and courts.*

As you read, consider the following questions:

1. How does the author support his claim that violations of the New Jersey graduated licensing law are not being punished?

2. As stated by Davis, why do law enforcement officials state that the graduated licensing law is difficult to enforce on the road?

3. What inaccurate assumption do parents make, in Pam Fischer's view?

Teenage traffic deaths have jumped 16 percent since a law was enacted in 2001 to safeguard young drivers. New Jersey's graduated driver's license [GDL] was intended to restrict when 16- and 17-year-olds can drive and who can be their passengers. The idea was to bring young drivers along at a slower pace, letting them gain experience behind the wheel with more adult supervision.

But now parents, police and lawmakers and a state task force are questioning whether changes in driver training and lax enforcement of the law have contributed to the increase in deaths.

Their concerns include:

• School districts have eliminated nearly 90 percent of their free behind-the-wheel driver education programs since the 1970s.

• Parents are not teaching the rules of the road to their children or setting examples of responsible behavior.

• State agencies and court systems are too overburdened to handle GDL cases.

• Barely 60 percent of those ticketed for violating the GDL law are convicted of the offense. Many plea bargain to a lesser charge. On average in 2006, 15 tickets per town were issued for violating the GDL law.

"Out of the challenges we face comes the opportunity to make important changes," Governor [Jon] Corzine said after signing legislation in March [2007] establishing the Teen Driver Study Commission.

Indeed, recklessness and neglect were motivating factors in a Freehold car crash that killed four people, three of them teens, in January, authorities say. The 17-year-old driver had a provisional license, but he violated the GDL by carrying one too many passengers, authorities said.

Also in January, a 17-year-old driver involved in a crash in Wayne that killed his two teenage passengers was charged with vehicular homicide.

Though the 15-member commission has yet to convene—Corzine's near-fatal accident has delayed the appointment process—the tragedies inspired lawmakers, law enforcement officers and traffic safety advocates to reexamine teen driving standards. All plan to take an active role in the commission's work.

"There could be factors we're not looking at that need to be addressed," said Assemblyman John Wisniewski, D-Middlesex, chairman of the Transportation and Public Works Committee.

"Not Making a Dent"

What's ironic is that New Jersey has one of the toughest GDL laws in the nation, said David Weinstein, a spokesman for AAA Mid-Atlantic. But while states like California have had declines in traffic fatalities, New Jersey is "not making a dent," he said.

In 2001, the year the GDL was enacted, New Jersey ranked 30th in traffic fatalities involving 16- and 17-year-olds.

In 2005—the most recent year available—it was 24th, according to the National Highway Traffic Safety Administration. Fatalities—79 in 2005—have risen back to the high levels of the early 1990s, when teen-driver crashes spiked and inspired the creation of the GDL. The increase in fatalities outpaced population growth.

"The thing that's missing is an understanding of what it [the law] is and how it can be enforced," Weinstein said. State officials, traffic safety advocates and even teenagers acknowledge that many flout the law, carrying too many passengers or driving all hours of the day.

"It's easy to get to places you want to go to," said Aisha Balado, a 17-year-old Bogota High School sophomore who has a provisional driver's license.

Teen drivers convicted of moving violations that carry two or more points can have their license suspended and be required to go to driver training, said Mike Horan, a spokesman for the Motor Vehicle Commission.

Law enforcement officials, however, say it's difficult to fully enforce the law because it would require police officers to question every driver who looks like a teenager, and to determine if they're carrying too many passengers. Under the law, only one additional person from outside a motorist's household is allowed in the vehicle.

Teaching the Parents

Parents also don't help by trusting teenagers too much and assuming they'll drive responsibly when they hand them the keys.

Pam Fischer, director of the state Division of Highway Traffic Safety, said many parents assume that all children should know how to operate a vehicle once they complete driver education training.

"But I say [to them], 'Wait a minute it takes about 1,000 hours of driving before the numbers [of accidents and other issues] go down,'" she said.

Restrictions Have Not Done Enough

The first teen graduated-license programs started in the mid-1990s. By 2003, 47 states had them. And during that period, the fatal crash rate for 16-year-olds dropped 34 percent, according to a 2005 study by the Insurance Institute [for Highway Safety].

Despite the drop, auto-safety researchers say the restrictions have not done enough to reduce teen crashes. Auto crashes are still the leading cause of death for 16- to 20-year-olds, according to the federal government. Police enforcement is difficult, and many teens—and their parents—ignore the restrictions, traffic-safety researchers and driver's education instructors say. And despite the growth of graduated-license laws over the last decade, the laws are weak in many states.

Sean Mussenden,
"Teen-Driving Laws Save Lives,"
Partners for Safe Teen Driving, May 17, 2006.

The New Jersey Police Traffic Officers Association has discussed making it easier to identify teen drivers by putting tags on their cars. But teens could still drive past midnight "by just using another car in the family," said Washington Township Police Chief William Cicchetti.

"It all goes back to teaching the parents and making sure they have the wherewithal to know all the rules and regulations," said Cicchetti, who heads the association.

Police officers also struggle to enforce the law because the Motor Vehicle Commission's [MVC's] 20-year-old computer system doesn't automatically track GDL violations, Cicchetti said.

Horan said the MVC will soon launch a multimillion-dollar project to update the agency's computer system by 2008. The updated system, he said, should properly track GDL offenses.

But Horan—echoing state officials—says updated technology won't fix a problem with teen driving that's proven to be overwhelming for state and local law enforcement agencies.

Plea Bargains

Nearly twice as many motorists were charged with GDL-related offenses from June 2006 to May 2007 compared with the same period in 2004 and 2005. But the state's overcrowded court system has been too merciful toward teen offenders, Horan said.

"There's nothing that prohibits plea agreements," said Tammy Kendig, a spokeswoman for the state Administrative Office of the Courts.

Lacking enforcement power, police officers and traffic-safety advocates have called for more education. Law enforcement officers and state officials including Fischer have held workshops and met with teenagers and parents to educate them on the GDL.

But Horan rejects calls that the MVC should take a more active role in regulating driving schools and even force school districts to provide more behind-the-wheel training.

"We're regulating junkyards. We're regulating auto body shops," he said. "We need to be dealing with teen driving. But we say, 'Shouldn't consumer affairs be doing this [junkyard and auto body] stuff?'"

Horan said he believes school districts could take a more active role and provide more than simple classroom instruction that "just teaches kids to [pass] the [written driving] test." New Jersey does not require behind-the-wheel training for new motorists who are 17 and older.

School districts, however, say they can no longer provide free behind-the-wheel training because it's too expensive—particularly with the high cost of liability insurance. Most eliminated their programs in the 1970s and 1980s.

State budget cuts in the 1990s also forced districts to scale back on programs that were considered unessential or unaffordable, said Mike Yaple, a spokesman for the New Jersey School Boards Association. Some, like Fair Lawn, send their students to outside driving schools.

"I think it would be a great idea to have it again, but it comes down to the fact that it's too expensive to run," said Sam Martone, a physical education teacher at Cliffside Park High School who helps run the school's classroom driver education program.

Ironically, the programs were dropped as more 16- and 17-year-olds have been buying cars and driving on their own, Yaple said. In Cliffside Park and other school districts, students must apply for parking permits because the lots at high schools are filling up every day.

Students, as a result, complain that they're forced to pay for expensive driving schools that charge as much as $300 to get training. Many don't bother, students say.

Jorelle Baker, 17, a Bogota High School junior has wanted to drive a car for a while so he can get to his job at Rite Aid on time. Instead, his 19-year-old sister drives him around. He's still tempted to get his provisional license, however.

"I don't have a permit, but I need a car. But it's [driver training] too expensive," he said.

Periodical Bibliography

The following articles have been selected to supplement the diverse views presented in this chapter.

David Bjerklie	"The Hidden Danger of Seat Belts," *TIME*, November 30, 2006.
Ron DeYoung	"Drunk Driving Penalties—Un-Constitutional?" *American Chronicle*, March 29, 2007.
Robyn Doolittle	"Does Street Racing Solution Lie on the Racetrack?" *Toronto Star*, October 9, 2007.
Jeff Gammage	"Car's 'Black Box' and What It Tells," *Philadelphia Inquirer*, November 24, 2007.
David Greig	"50th Anniversary of the 3-Point Seat Belt," *Gizmag*, February 26, 2009.
Bob Gritzinger	"Black Box on Board," *AutoWeek*, September 24, 2008.
Alexandra Marks	"Drunken Driving Is Down. But What About Drug Use by Drivers?" *Christian Science Monitor*, July 13, 2009.
Steve Parker	"Street Racing Kills—Help Me Stop It," *Huffing-ton Post*, July 22, 2008.
Matt Richtel	"Drivers and Legislators Dismiss Cellphone Risks," *New York Times*, July 18, 2009.

OPPOSING
VIEWPOINTS®
SERIES

CHAPTER 3

What Is the Future of the Car Industry in America?

Chapter Preface

In 2008, high gas prices, the global recession, and fierce competition from foreign automakers helped to create the perfect storm for the fall of the Big Three—Chrysler, Ford, and General Motors (GM). That November, the U.S. Senate held a hearing in which the Big Three requested $25 billion in federal funds to dodge bankruptcy. In early December, Chrysler, Ford, and GM submitted a revised plan asking for $34 billion. Chrysler asked for $7 billion and GM $4 billion to survive until the end of the year; Ford requested $9 billion in credit from the government and $5 billion from the U.S. Department of Energy.

On December 11, 2008, the Senate voted against the bailout. But eight days later, former president George W. Bush announced that he had approved a $13.4 billion bailout for Chrysler and GM. The former received $4 billion and the latter $9.4 billion. (GM would get an additional $4 billion in February 2009.) Under the agreement, the two companies were required to present long-term, profit-making business plans by March 31, 2009. Chrysler's chairman, Robert L. Nardelli, wrote in a company e-mail, "We intend to be accountable for this loan, including meeting the specific requirements set forth by the government, and will continue to implement our plan for long-term viability."[1] GM also moved forward and cut thirty thousand jobs, closed several plants, and began talks of discontinuing some of its brands.

The second round of auto bailouts began in February 2009. Chrysler and GM asked the government for an additional $21.6 billion in emergency funds. Both companies proposed slashing even more jobs—three thousand for Chrysler and forty-seven thousand for GM. Chrysler also said it would drop three of its models: the Aspen, PT Cruiser, and Durango. By the spring, GM stated that it would no longer produce or would sell off its Saab, Saturn, and HUMMER brands by the end of the 2009. Another brand, Pontiac, would be phased out in 2010. And in June, GM revealed that it would reduce its plants from forty-seven to thirty-three in the United States.

By the fall of that year, both automakers struggled with sagging sales. Lawmakers also raised the issue that Chrysler and GM made contract demands that would replace unionized with nonunionized workers. Nevertheless, *Brandweek* declared that the dire situation had improved for the Big Three in one respect—each had markedly increased its brand health score. In the following chapter, the authors examine the domestic auto crisis and the industry's future in America.

Notes

1. *New York Times*, December 19, 2008.

> "The United States needs a healthy do-
> mestic auto industry but for reasons
> that you may not have considered."

American Automakers Must Be Saved

John R. Dabels

In the following viewpoint, John R. Dabels contends that the 2008/2009 federal government bailout for struggling American automakers—Chrysler and General Motors (GM)—is necessary. Unlike the defense and aerospace sectors, Dabels asserts that large-scale automakers drive down the costs of technological advances. These innovations also have a wide array of applications, stimulating many other industries, he continues. Without the automobile industry, Dabels cautions that the fall in gross domestic product (GDP) and flagging technology would threaten national security. The author is chief executive of EV Power Systems and former marketing director of GM's electric vehicle program.

As you read, consider the following questions:

1. What does Dabels consider to be the core of the automobile industry?

2. What technological breakthrough does Dabels credit to GM?

3. How does the manufacturing capacity of a domestic automobile industry benefit national security, in the author's view?

In the last few months, the number of ordinary citizens, government officials and media pundits have asked, "Why should we use government money to bail out Chrysler and General Motors [GM]?" The comments continue, "Management has made bad decisions, UAW [United Auto Workers] wages are too high and no one wants to buy their cars. Besides, Toyota, Honda, Nissan, Hyundai and Mercedes[-Benz] all make vehicles in the United States."

The frustration is correct but the conclusion is not correct. The United States needs a healthy domestic auto industry but for reasons that you may not have considered.

Why am I writing this article? I'm writing because a number of people have asked me to. Once I explained my views, most said, "I never realized how important a domestic auto industry was."

What makes me an expert? My comments are based on some fundamental laws of economics and 40 plus years in the auto business with experience inside a large auto company and experience starting a hybrid-electric vehicle company. I've been in technology centers, on factory floors, in boardrooms, in dealerships, in design centers and in dealership service bays. I've been involved with some good, some bad and some ugly projects.

So why is a successful domestic auto industry so important? I think three fundamental reasons: (i) ensuring advanced technology is readily available (ii) stimulating growth in other industries (iii) helping ensure national security.

What makes the auto industry different from most other industries is a combination of large scale, complex manufacturing and demands for extremely high levels of reliability and durability, especially compared to other products. Everyone I have ever met who entered the auto industry after time in another industry makes the same comment after 2-3 weeks, "The auto business is much more complicated than I realized." And the comment usually includes several expletives.

The degree of complexity does not mean "outsiders" should not enter the industry. Far from it. But outsiders need to be cautious about ignoring staff who have toiled inside the companies for many years. Intuitional knowledge is very valuable and should not be taken lightly. Clean the water and be careful with the babies.

Ensuring Availability of Advanced Technology

What does the auto industry do that cannot be done by the defense or aircraft industry? The answer is scale. Large scale drives down cost and low cost makes products affordable for many more consumers. While much new technology is developed in defense and aerospace industries, neither industry generates the volume necessary to drive down cost.

Think about the number of military and civilian aircraft built each year. The total number built for the entire year is equal to about one day's production at one auto plant. And there are more than 20 auto assembly plants in the United States. Auto companies produce 15-16,000,000 new cars and trucks in every year, just for the U.S. market.

Thus, for technology to be introduced in cars and trucks—even very expensive ones—cost must drop 1 to 2 orders of magnitude, or more than 90%, from cost acceptable for a defense or aerospace application.

Further, parts on cars must function with essentially no maintenance. Think about how little you maintain your car or truck vs. the number of miles or hours you drive. Yes, you may refuel but how often do you change oil, have a tune-up or overhaul the engine compared to miles driven? Would you fly on a commercial airplane with the same maintenance schedule as you have for your car? Of course not.

Despite the limited maintenance schedule, cars and trucks are expected to operate and last 15–20 years, or more. What other major piece of equipment so widely used in so many different environments lasts that long?

Well, you say, I still don't understand why we need to bail out GM and Chrysler. As a point of clarification, when I talk about the auto industry, I mean more than just assembly plants. The core of the auto industry is primarily component design and manufacturing. The assembly plants get all the glamour but industry guts are in components—electronics, robots, batteries, wheels, frames, tires, steering, foundries for engines and brakes and many other components.

Manufacturing components is where the value is created and where knowledge gained can be transferred to other industries. As a country we often overlook the need to remain competitive in producing components. The United States does not need to produce all components for all cars made in the United States. But is does need to maintain the capability of producing a high percentage of each key component.

Stimulating Other Industries

The technology used in autos is directly applicable to many other industries. The demands of the auto design and manufacturing force many suppliers to improve their own technology. A strong domestic auto industry increases the likelihood, although does not ensure, the United States is creating, receiving and utilizing the latest technology.

Will foreign auto companies with U.S. assembly plants transfer the latest technology to the United States? No. Just as the U.S.-companies do not export their latest technology to other countries. If there is any question about countries keeping technology at home first, one should study technology

Backs to the Wall

Two overarching considerations, however, should shape our thinking [about the Big Three]:

First, the global macroeconomic and financial crisis is so staggering that even the healthiest auto companies have their backs to the wall. Global auto sales are in a free fall, pushing Toyota to its first losses in history. This would be a near-death experience even for companies with stronger balance sheets. All over the world, the industry is receiving state aid.

Second, and perhaps most important, however, is that the Big Three have a future as industry leaders in 21st century transport, but can't get there on their own. We are entering a new age of Sustainable Capitalism, in which our most central technological systems—in energy production and use, building codes, land use, food production, water management, and ecosystem conservation—will be fundamentally overhauled to reflect the dramatically intensifying scarcity or degradation of environmental resources. In every major sphere of the economy, new technologies will replace existing technologies in order to reconcile high living standards with environmental sustainability and national security (for example, related to Middle East oil).

Jeffrey Sachs,
"How to Bring Back the Big 3,"
Fortune, *February 17, 2009.*

available in cars sold by Toyota and Nissan in Japan compared to technology available in the United States. Frequently the technology is not available in the United States for 2 to 3 years after being introduced in Japan.

Further, some technology breakthroughs have a long-lasting impact. An example is the effort by GM in the early 1990s to develop and introduce an electric vehicle, EV1. While GM was praised for introducing the car, and skewered when stopping production, the advances and electronics developed for the EV1 program were the foundation for many electronics available in cars and trucks today, nearly 20 years after the EV1 concept car was introduced at the Los Angeles Auto Show.

Yes, GM deserves criticism for canceling the program. But GM deserves praise for advancing automotive electronics, which in turn led to the use of advanced electronics in many non-automotive applications. The strong domestic auto industry creates advancements in technology that benefit the auto industry and all segments of industry and everyday consumers.

Advanced technology applied in non-auto industries keeps U.S. companies competitive worldwide. Exports create jobs. If you think transportation-driven technology is not important to other industries, think about productivity in agriculture, raw materials, manufacturing, distribution and other industries. Most of the productivity gains were greatly influenced by demands first met in the auto industry. Without such productivity, the U.S. output and incomes would fall toward lesser developed nations.

Yes, I know, Silicon Valley is great. But the country needs to translate the ideas to generate wealth for the United States. Manufacturing generates wealth, services do not. Computers that move information around are not the same as computers used to increase efficiency in manufacturing. Knowledge without manufacturing does not create wealth.

National Security

Since foreign-based auto companies do not transfer the latest technology—and why should they—the United States will fall behind in technology development for everyday products and manufacturing efficiencies. This in turn will lower potential GDP [gross domestic product] growth and personal incomes.

More importantly, however, without a higher-volume domestic auto industry to spread cost, will the country be able to afford the cost for developing new technology used primarily for defense and aerospace applications? Probably not unless we raise taxes and lower incomes.

Finally, and let's hope this never occurs again, but what happens if the United States needs manufacturing capacity for a large-scale ground war? A domestic auto industry, both assembly and component manufacturers will be critical for rapid conversion from automotive production to defense material. Having only assembly plants without domestically sourced components—engines, transmissions, axles, electronics, and so forth—offers no benefit for national security.

Sourcing components manufactured outside the United States has an equal, if not greater, potential negative impact on national security and technology advancement than the assembly of vehicles in the United States.

Smart Investment

Taxpayer dollars to ensure a vibrant domestic auto assembly and component manufacturing industry are dollars well spent—a smart investment. What would the hue and cry be from these same critics of GM and Chrysler if the defense and aerospace industries began outsourcing critical defense weapons systems to such countries as India, China and Japan?

If you still have doubts, name one country worldwide that has sustained growth in GDP and real growth in consumer incomes without a strong manufacturing base built around the strong automobile industry? Call me when you can name one. Supporting a strong domestic automobile industry is smart economics. Charles E. Wilson was correct, when he said many years ago, "What is good for General Motors is good for the country and vice versa."

2

> "A prepackaged bankruptcy actually
> could leave the major automakers in
> better shape than they were prior to
> the financial crisis."

American Automakers Should Not Be Saved

Dan Weil

In the following viewpoint, Dan Weil maintains that several lies and misperceptions were used to promote the 2008/2009 government bailout of Chrysler and General Motors (GM). American autoworkers are not undercompensated, Weil argues, and the American automobile industry is not unique. Furthermore, the author proposes that bankruptcy would help, not doom, the industry and the government aid package cannot sustain Chrysler and GM in the long run. In fact, he blames American automakers for not adjusting to the changing marketplace or competition. Weil is a contributor to Newsmax.com, a conservative news Web site.

As you read, consider the following questions:

1. How have automobile industry supporters distorted domestic workers' wages, in Weil's opinion?

2. What is the importance of the state of the newspaper industry to the author?

3. As described by Weil, what set apart the government bailout of Chrysler in 1980?

With congressional Democrats and the [George W.] Bush administration agreeing in principle during the weekend [in December 2008] to drop a few billion on General Motors and Chrysler, all signs point to a government-backed auto industry bailout. But could the crisis in Detroit be the product of myth, spin and outright lies?

As the nation inches closer to an unprecedented investment in private industry, Newsmax has examined the falsehoods being spread to promote the deal. Indeed, the exact amount of money to be doled out isn't clear yet. GM and Chrysler executives testified before Congress last week that they need $14 billion to survive until March 31.

Whatever the total, a number of financial experts say it would be money better left unspent until the Big Three and their supporters agree to level with the American taxpayers. Until the carmakers can offer convincing proof that they will be able to produce cars at a reasonable price that customers will want to buy, here are four of the biggest whoppers they are relying on to get a massive infusion of American tax dollars:

1. Detroit's Wages Really Aren't Out of Sync with Those of Autoworkers in Other Countries.

It has been well established that total compensation for U.S. autoworkers, including pensions and benefits, comes in around $70 per hour. That compares to $45 per hour for Japanese workers.

But some auto industry supporters have distorted the argument. They use the American workers' hourly wage without benefits—about $30 an hour—and compare that number to the $45 hourly total compensation for Japanese workers. Then they claim that U.S. automakers are actually more labor efficient than their Japanese counterparts.

Obviously that's not comparing apples to apples. If you are looking at apples versus apples, a new auto plant in India offers hourly pay of only $19.

And it's not just line workers who are overpaid. Ford's chief executive Alan Mulally earned $22 million in total compensation last year—a year that helped push the company toward oblivion. Asked last month if he thought he deserved a pay cut, Mulally said, "I think I'm all right where I am."

Top executives at Bear Stearns, AIG, Lehman Brothers, and Merrill Lynch probably felt the same way right before their companies went under.

2. The Auto Industry Is Unique and Therefore Must Be Bailed Out.

It's true that auto companies, including suppliers, etc., account for about 3 percent of economic output and employ at least 1 million people. But those numbers aren't dependent on the financial status of the Big Three.

If the companies go into bankruptcy and come out stronger, the industry will employ about the same amount of people. If not, foreign automakers will produce more cars in the United States and pick up many of these workers.

Plenty other uniquely American industries are taking it on the chin, and no one is calling for a bailout of those sectors. Take newspapers for example. One could argue they are far more important for the functioning of our democracy than the Big Three auto companies.

Newspapers are firing workers right and left and shifting more of their operations to the Internet. And they will have to continue doing so until they can put out a news product cheaply enough and well enough so that readers will pay to read it, and advertisers will pay to appear in it.

Eroding Investment

Will fewer companies look to insource into America if the federal government is willing to bail out their domestic competitors?

The answer is an obvious yes. Ironically, proponents of a bailout say saving Detroit is necessary to protect the U.S. manufacturing base. But too many such bailouts could erode the number of manufacturers willing to invest here.

Matthew J. Slaughter,
"An Auto Bailout Would Be Terrible for Free Trade,"
Wall Street Journal, *November 20, 2008.*

That's called adjusting to a changed marketplace, something the Big Three have largely failed to do since first facing foreign competition in the 1970s.

3. Bankruptcy for the Big Three Will Mean the End of the U.S. Auto Industry.

That is simply poppycock. A prepackaged bankruptcy actually could leave the major automakers in better shape than they were prior to the financial crisis. Since the mid-1990s, the Big Three made most of their money on gas-guzzling SUVs [sport utility vehicles] and trucks. That simply won't cut it anymore. Bankruptcy will force the automakers to quicken their shift to smaller cars.

Plenty of companies have emerged stronger from bankruptcy. Nearly all the major airlines have gone through that process and came out stronger than when they entered. Some industry apologists have argued that American consumers won't buy any cars from the Big Three if they are in bankruptcy because of concern that warranties won't be honored.

But as long as the companies offer quality autos at reasonable prices and make it clear that warranties will remain in place no matter what happens to the companies themselves, American drivers will want the cars.

Meanwhile, bankruptcy would give the Big Three an opportunity to rework their labor contracts, cutting compensation, and to jettison incompetent executives.

4. A Limited Aid Package Now Will Ensure the Industry's Long-Term Future.

The amount of money being bandied about, $15 billion to $25 billion, is chump change. GM and Chrysler are bleeding $2 billion in cash a month. So the high end of the bailout range keeps them in business for about a year. Then what? Without major changes in their business model, they'll simply be coming back to Washington with their hands out again.

The Big Three have had so many opportunities to change their practices since the first oil crisis of the early 1970s, yet they have been reluctant to budge. GM still has eight brands of cars, even though critics have pointed out for years that's probably about seven too many.

As recently as last month, GM CEO [chief executive officer] Rick Wagoner had the gall to tell Congress: "What exposes us to failure now is not our product lineup, or our business plan, or our long-term strategy."

Until Wagoner and others at the Big Three come to realize those are exactly the factors that have put the industry on the brink of failure, there is no hope for improvement. And it's not a bailout that's going to make auto companies implement the adjustments they need to survive.

And remember, this current "bailout" bears no resemblance to the rescue of Chrysler in 1980. In 1980, Congress passed, and President [Jimmy] Carter signed, a law giving a U.S. government guarantee of a private $1.5 billion loan to Chrysler. Not one dollar of taxpayer funds was ever used in the deal. It's also important to remember that import tariffs sheltered Chrysler and the Big Three from Japanese competition in the 1980s. And unlike today, Chrysler also had a clear plan to make a comeback and the loan was relatively small.

All of the automakers should follow Chrysler's 1980s success story: Create a viable business plan for the future and get private sources to fund it.

"A new generation of auto entrepreneurs
is rising, committed to building greener
modes of transportation in new ways."

Gas-Electric Hybrids and Electric Cars Will Transform the Car Industry in America

Peter Grier and Mark Clayton

Peter Grier and Mark Clayton are staff writers for the Christian
Science Monitor. *In the following viewpoint, Grier and Clayton
claim that American carmakers dedicated to developing greener
vehicles will change the nation's automobile industry. Small
start-ups, such as Bright Automotive, that are honing hybrid and
electric-motor technologies and other techniques may just build
the next-generation automobile, the authors propose. Moreover,
they say that traditional carmakers in Detroit are making relative headway with their own hybrids, such as Ford's Fusion and
General Motors' Volt. Grier and Clayton also predict that the
global automobile industry—with growing demands for affordable cars in developing countries—is set to take off.*

As you read, consider the following questions:

1. What happened to General Motors' EV1, the first mass-produced electric car, according to Grier and Clayton?

2. As stated by Grier and Clayton, what are some future U.S. policies on hybrid and fuel efficiency?

3. Why is India's Nano a success, in the authors' opinion?

John Waters is leaning against a vehicle that looks like a delivery van as imagined by Pixar Animation. The IDEA—that's its name—is blocky, yet curved, with wheel skirts and a little upswoop at the back that adds attitude. You can almost hear it speaking in a chirpy cartoon voice.

Inside IDEA's silver sheet metal is plug-in hybrid technology that will power it an estimated 100 miles on a gallon of gas. If Mr. Waters has his way, thousands of these cuddly vans will soon be double-parked all across America, blocking travel lanes while their drivers wait for someone—anyone!—to sign for these darn packages, please.

Years ago Waters worked on General Motors' legendary EV1 electric car program. Now he's president and CEO [chief executive officer] of Bright Automotive, an Anderson, Ind., start-up that's recruited many EV1 veterans to help develop a new generation of hybrid trucks and cars.

"It's the wealth of experience of our people that will make this work," he says.

A New Generation

One hundred and one years after the debut of the Model T, the automobile—and the iconic industry that produces it—may be on the cusp of changes as profound as any ever wrought by Henry Ford.

Detroit is in crisis. The Big Three is no more. In the wake of recession, GM's [General Motors'] and Chrysler's bankruptcies, and Chrysler's merger with Fiat, the traditional Michigan-based automakers now might better be called the Medium Two and One-Half.

Meanwhile, a new generation of auto entrepreneurs is rising, committed to building greener modes of transportation in new ways. They're scrambling for billions in government aid intended to jump-start production of vehicles that burn little gasoline—or no gasoline at all.

Plus—and this sounds odd, given the current emptiness of U.S. showrooms—the auto industry may be about to see its biggest growth spurt ever. Developed nations choke on traffic, but in the rest of the world hundreds of millions of consumers yearn for their first set of wheels.

Brazil, Russia, China, India, and Indonesia are among the rapidly emerging countries where per capita incomes are at or near the level at which auto ownership typically takes off. Consulting firm Booz & Company predicts the world will have 1.5 billion cars in use in 2018, up from 672 million today.

Who will produce those vehicles? What will they look like? These questions will help shape some of the industries of tomorrow, and, along with them, the economies of nations. For now, new firms such as China's Geely and India's Tata are now rising to challenge the founding titans of the horseless carriage.

"The global auto industry is still developing," says Bruce Belzowski, an associate director at the University of Michigan's Transportation Research Institute. "In five to 10 years, there could be strong competition on a global scale."

The Beat of the Electronic Heart

Anderson is one of those Midwestern towns where modern automobile technology was born. Flint, Mich., had its engine and body shops, and Detroit its production lines, but Anderson provided cars with the beat of their electronic heart.

By 1900, Anderson was home to 11 automakers and two brothers, Perry and Frank Remy, whose Remy Electric would soon become the nation's leading producer of magnetos and dynamos needed to start cars in the nation's growing auto fleet.

Through the decades, legions of electrical engineers worked at Remy and at other nearby manufacturers to develop power for lights, radios, seat warmers, keyless remote entry fobs, and computer-controlled engine and ventilation systems. Anderson and the rest of central Indiana was the "Silicon Valley" of vehicles, says William Wylam, a former director at Delco Remy, Remy's successor firm.

That's "was," as in, "isn't any longer." Today Anderson, a city of 60,000 northeast of Indianapolis, mixes run-down bungalows and shuttered storefronts against the backdrop of an empty 1960s-era headlight factory. "Everything here in Anderson today is gone—it's all gone and most of the [factory] buildings are torn down," says Mr. Wylam.

Well, maybe not everything. A little company out by the state highway, Wylam adds, is mining the area's biggest remaining resource—its rich vein of human talent.

That firm is Bright Automotive. A number of its key people used to work at GM's Indianapolis research center, which developed the EV1, the first modern production electric vehicle from a major automaker. Introduced in 1996, the EV1 was available in California and Arizona, via lease. GM discontinued it in 1999, citing program expense. It recalled the cars. Most of them were crushed. But the EV1 engineers' dreams weren't crushed with them.

"These are highly qualified, highly motivated people," says Wylam. "I wouldn't want to get in their way."

The IDEA is Bright's main project. Working from a gleaming office park on the edge of Anderson, the Bright team has put together a prototype of the vehicle, which combines plug-in hybrid technology with extensive use of aluminum, carbon fiber, and other weight-reduction techniques.

Regular hybrids, like today's Toyota Prius, use an electric motor and a small internal combustion engine. Plug-in hybrids use that technology, too, but with a big battery and big electric motor, plus—surprise!—a plug. They also recharge their batteries by plugging into the regular electric grid.

Waters says the IDEA will get around 100 miles of city driving for every gallon of gas. It's van-size because the company figures it could win over bean counters at companies pressed by high fuel costs, such as FedEx, UPS, and the U.S. Postal Service.

But if the company is to turn out 50,000 of these swoopy things a year by 2012, as it plans, it needs cash—and today investment dollars are hard to come by. So Bright has turned to the federal government. The firm has applied for $35 million in grants from the stimulus bill, as well as a $450 million loan from a Department of Energy green technology program.

Bright is hardly the only U.S. firm with an idea like IDEA. At least a half-dozen start-up companies, with names like Aptera and Visionary Vehicles, are vying for funding to build the next-generation automobile.

Many—probably most—won't survive. That shouldn't be surprising, as firms rose and fell in the early years of the internal combustion engine, too. Who today remembers the Mercer Raceabout, or Essex, or Nash Statesman? All were cutting-edge cars in their heyday. But their heydays all turned out to be brief.

Nothing Is Certain

Of course, nothing is certain about the auto industry these days. It is shaking to its very foundations. Toyota is losing money. A niche Swedish sports-car maker has bought country icon Saab. HUMMER has become less fashionable than Hyundai. Chrysler's next model may be based on the Fiat 500, a car so small that it looks like a Dodge Charger's lunch.

Then there is General Motors, ward of the state. Those who remember GM as the producer of such iconographic autos as the 1957 Bel Air may see its fall as a shame. Those who bought the awful 1970s Chevy Monza (or its evil twin, the Oldsmobile Starfire) may consider its bankruptcy well deserved.

The U.S. government has already invested some $80 billion in tax dollars in GM and Chrysler. It probably will be at least a year before the Treasury can even begin to plan when it might sell government-owned shares in the company to recoup that cash.

Will the United States ever get that money back? There are "reasonable scenarios" under which the taxpayer investment will be returned, said Ron Bloom, President [Barack] Obama's high-profile auto adviser, at a June 10 [2009] Senate hearing. "But by no means would I say that I am highly confident that will occur."

That does not sound like a ringing endorsement, does it? Post-bankruptcy, both GM and Chrysler will be shorn of debt and overhead, and theoretically will be better able to compete in a tough market. The key may be to what point U.S. sales recover.

In January, the pace of vehicle sales in America fell below 10 million units annually for the first time in almost three decades. Some analysts see sales staying in a trough for years, as newly frugal consumers learn to do without leased Audi Q7s, and turn to the used-car market, or (gasp!) keep driving their old cars instead.

Others think that is too pessimistic. In the United States, about 13 million cars a year are scrapped due to advanced age, according to the International Motor Vehicle Program [IMVP], a research consortium founded at the Massachusetts Institute of Technology in 1979. (Aren't the Monzas all gone by now?)

That loss might put a floor under demand. "The global auto industry will recover to pre-crisis levels as the global economy recovers: There is no paradigm shift at hand," says a recent research paper from the IMVP, a nonprofit funded by donations from auto firms, as well as other sources.

A Little Greener

Post-trough, the U.S. auto industry at least will look a little greener. Besides start-ups, the traditional U.S. automakers are moving to hybrid models. Ford's new Fusion hybrid is doing well in showrooms today, relatively speaking. GM is making a big deal out of its forthcoming Chevy Volt, an extended-range plug-in hybrid that will be available next year.

Mr. Obama wants 1 million plug-in hybrids on U.S. roads by 2015. By 2016, the United States will require automakers to produce fleets of vehicles that get an average of 35.5 miles per gallon, up from today's figure of 27.5. The federal government is poised to spend billions on everything from new lithium-battery plants to incentives for consumers to buy more-efficient cars.

A new generation of electric cars, as a result, is moving toward showrooms. In the United States, 13 hybrid models were available in 2007. By 2011, at least 75 will be on dealer lots, Deutsche Bank reported last year. IHS Global Insight, a consulting firm, projects 47 percent hybridization of the U.S. market by 2020. In Europe, where fuel economy requirements are tougher, the transition could be even more dramatic: Roland Berger and J.D. Power estimate that the market for hybrids/electric vehicles could rise to 50 percent by 2015—up from 2 percent in 2007.

Is the gas-powered V-8 about to become as extinct as 8-track tapes?

"What we are seeing today is a major shift toward electric-drive vehicles," says Dan Sperling, director of the Institute of Transportation Studies at the University of California, Davis.

The End of "Horsepower Wars"

It may take a few years, but as automakers invest their engineering talent in more efficient cars and new technologies—rather than "horsepower wars," the competitive mantra of the past dozen years—the payoff will be cars that do more and require less fuel. It will be a painful transition for drivers and car companies alike. But the car you drive 10 years from now might just be a prototype for the gas-free automobile.

Rick Newman,
"What GM's Downsizing Means for Drivers,"
U.S. News & World Report, June 3, 2008.

Well, maybe. Other experts point out that Obama's goal of 1 million hybrids is quite modest, given that even in this constrained year U.S. consumers will drive away 9 million new vehicles.

Habits and Costs

The problems are habits, and costs. Consumers have been driving gas cars—and big ones, in the United States—for a century. Most of them are not going to pay more to try something new.

And electric-drive cars are more expensive, at least for now. Batteries are costly, for one thing. Chevy's Volt will probably have a sticker price near $40,000. Unless government policy offsets this green price penalty, hybrids and their ilk could remain a niche product in the short to medium term.

"In five years, if fuel prices don't do anything crazy, the product mix will look pretty much like it does today," says Daniel Snow, an assistant professor at Harvard Business School who studies the application of new technology.

Gas prices might do something crazy, of course. They've roller-coastered quite a bit recently. At last summer's $4 per gallon, consumers fled big vehicles. Hybrids were hot—but so were four-cylinder economy cars. And, technically speaking, conventional gas autos still have lots of leeway for mileage improvement. Direct fuel injection, use of lighter weight materials, and other techniques could improve efficiency by 20 percent or more.

"There isn't any part of the vehicle that will remain untouched by the search for better mileage," says Paul Lacy, manager of technical research, Global Automotive Group, at IHS Global Insight.

In the longer run, the power source of a vehicle may depend on its intended use. Runabout cars for shopping and school drop-offs could be straight electric. Commuter vehicles that take longer trips downtown might need the extended-range capability of a hybrid. Long-distance cruisers meant to travel at high speeds from, say, Tucson, Ariz., to Tucumcari, New Mexico, might operate best with advanced diesel-fueled spark-ignition engines.

Cars, in other words, will still be around—for a long time. That is easy to forget now, particularly in the United States, as GM stumbles and the price of gas heads for its next unpredictable destination. Mass transit is great, but the auto is one of history's revolutionary technologies. People everywhere want the freedom inherent in a personal set of wheels.

Emerging from Infancy

Given the number of people in the developing world who can now afford a basic auto, or will soon be able to, the global vehicle industry may not yet have seen its period of greatest growth. "The motor vehicle manufacturing industry, which is 100 years old, is only now emerging from its infancy," conclude Ronald Haddock and John Jullens, analysts at Booz & Company, in a recent report.

Once a nation's gross domestic product reaches $10,000 per capita, its rate of automobile ownership accelerates, according to Booz & Company data. Among those countries that have not yet reached that point, but will soon, are Russia, India, China, Malaysia, Indonesia, and Iran.

The bottom line: Even given the recession, world auto sales could total 715 million units over the next nine years. And the most important attribute a car can have in this new global market may not be electric drive or plug-in technology, but low expense. When a farmer from rural China goes looking to upgrade from his motorbike, the first thing he'll look for is something he can afford.

That is why the Tata Nano is such a big deal. It is the world's cheapest production car, with a price tag of about $2,500. No, its trunk does not open. (Access is from the inside.) Engineers shaved costs by attaching wheels with three lug nuts, instead of four. It looks like a beanbag chair, or possibly a large kitchen appliance. But when its Indian manufacturer, Tata Motors, began taking orders for the car this spring, it sold 200,000 in 16 days.

Demand for low-priced vehicles around the world soon will be huge, says Hiroshi Hasegawa, president of SC-ABeam Automotive Consulting in Tokyo. And that business may not go to Buick or Volkswagen or Toyota. Even in Japan, young adults now covet cell phones as status items but see cars as simply a way to get around. "I would expect Chinese and Indian low-priced cars to meet such demand," says Mr. Hasegawa.

In the 1970s, Japanese automakers invaded the United States and Western Europe with efficient small cars, tapping a market the locals did not know existed. Now, those same manufacturers may be planning for a different kind of global competition, in which many more firms than before take part. "We expect to move into a multipolar age," says Hasegawa.

And what part of this market do the Japanese want to pre-dominate in? Yep—hybrids and other electric-drive vehicles. Toyota and Honda beat U.S. firms to the marketplace with hybrids, and they are not eager to cede that ground to anyone— even an eager upstart like Bright Automotive, with its friendly 100-mile-per-gallon van.

Toyota expects that by 2020, hybrids will account for more than 20 percent of its annual sales volume.

"Japanese carmakers acquired technologies and production know-how on [hybrids and electric vehicles] a long time ago," says Koji Endo, an auto analyst with Credit Suisse in Tokyo. "They will continue to improve their techniques while cutting costs in the next five years."

Takehiko Kambayashi contributed from Tokyo.

> *"Even if Detroit overcomes decades of consumer skepticism about the quality of its products and begins cranking out fuel-efficient cars that don't damage the environment—even then the U.S. auto industry could die."*

Gas-Electric Hybrids and Electric Cars Will Not Transform the Car Industry in America

Jim Tankersley

Jim Tankersley is a reporter based in Washington, D.C. In the following viewpoint, he states that revitalizing America's automobile industry will require much more than a shift to greener, more fuel-efficient cars. First, Tankersley upholds that demand for high-mileage vehicles has historically depended on skyrocketing oil prices. Second, the author suggests that Chrysler, Ford, and General Motors must produce cars that have consumer appeal and must catch up to the quality standards of foreign carmakers. Thus, he concludes that coercive efficiency policies for Detroit will not be enough.

As you read, consider the following questions:

1. How does Tankersley compare gas-electric hybrids to luxury automobiles?

2. According to the author, what is the Barack Obama administration's main critique of Chrysler, Ford, and General Motors?

3. What is Robert Murphy's position on the push for more fuel-efficient cars?

President [Barack] Obama's threat to cut off government loans and bring on bankruptcy has given him unprecedented leverage to realize his vision of Detroit as the world leader in greener cars.

Yet even if the president succeeds in getting domestic carmakers onto firmer financial ground, even if Detroit overcomes decades of consumer skepticism about the quality of its products and begins cranking out fuel-efficient cars that don't damage the environment—even then the U.S. auto industry could die.

Discussions about what must happen for General Motors, Chrysler and Ford to survive have centered on issues such as reducing labor costs and persuading creditors to scale down the companies' debts.

Beyond that, Obama said recently: "This restructuring, as painful as it will be in the short term, will mark not an end but a new beginning for a great American industry . . . that is creating new jobs, unleashing new prosperity and manufacturing the fuel-efficient cars and trucks that will carry us toward an energy-independent future."

Two Factors

For that vision to be realized, economists and marketing specialists say, offering cars that are greener and get better mileage is not enough. Two other factors will be important in deciding Detroit's fate.

First, oil prices must take off. High-mileage, low-pollution vehicles generally cost more, and demand for them historically has jumped in times of rapidly rising gas prices and faded when fuel becomes less expensive.

Second, the cars Detroit produces must satisfy consumer tastes and preferences. Marketing data show that a vehicle's size and the image it bestows on its driver play major roles in buyers' decisions.

Reflecting those factors, the two most popular import luxury brands, Mercedes-Benz and BMW, snagged nearly 4% of the U.S. auto market in March [2009], selling more than 33,000 cars. That's about 12,000 more vehicles—and a 50% larger market share—than all hybrids combined.

In other words, greener and more efficient alone will not ensure a bright future for Detroit.

"You will not get people to buy more fuel-efficient cars unless gas prices go up," said Howard Wial, a fellow at the Brookings Institution in Washington who studies the auto industry. Moreover, he said, "whether the Detroit Three will be the ones to sell those cars . . . really depends on their own innovative capacity."

Case in point: When gas approached $4 a gallon last year, consumers who formerly bought Mercedes and BMWs flocked to the Toyota Prius hybrid—for its lower operating cost, sleek styling and high-tech features—said Alexander Edwards, automotive president for the marketing firm Strategic Vision.

Those companies "could take the idea of green and use it to enhance other psychological factors that customers were looking for. . . . [If] you have a sexy, attractive hybrid vehicle, or something innovative like the Prius, that's going to work."

Today, however, with oil selling well off its peak and the economy in the doldrums, Priuses are a glut on the market.

Patterns Repeat Themselves

At the heart of the Obama administration's critique of GM [General Motors], Chrysler and Ford is the idea that they lost a once-dominant hold on the American automobile market because they kept building SUVs [sport utility vehicles] and other gas-guzzlers instead of the efficient cars customers wanted. In addition, administration officials and environmentalists contend that global warming and a dependence on foreign oil require shifting away from vehicles powered by petroleum.

History shows that's difficult. Since the 1973 Arab oil embargo, a pattern has repeated itself: Disruptions in world markets—engineered by producers or caused by events such as wars in the Persian Gulf region—drive gasoline prices skyward. Consumers respond by looking for cars that inflict less pain at the pump. And every time prices level off, the demand for smaller, more efficient cars fades.

But Detroit automakers long ignored signs that higher fuel prices would shift demand, said Walter McManus, an economist at the University of Michigan's Transportation Research Institute and former sales forecaster for GM.

McManus said he and other GM analysts tweaked projection models when they didn't believe their results.

"We thought we were smarter than consumers," he said— particularly in regard to fuel economy, the impact of which they minimized "in a way we would never [minimize] horsepower or cup holders."

Japanese and European automakers didn't have that option. High gas taxes in their home markets kept fuel prices up and forced them to concentrate on more efficient cars. They beat their American rivals to hybrid technology and to smaller SUVs.

The gas price increases from 2002 to 2007 explain about 40% of U.S. auto manufacturers' lost market share, according to researchers from the University of Illinois at Chicago and the Federal Reserve Board of Chicago.

American carmakers fell behind in other key measures too. Starting in the early 1970s, they "missed the signals that they were vulnerable in the long term because the cars they were producing weren't delivering the quality that other firms, like Toyota, were producing," said Jorge Silva-Risso, an associate marketing professor at UC [University of California] Riverside who specializes in auto sales.

Detroit has caught up on some quality standards, other analysts said, but still lags in areas such as noise, vibration and smoothness of ride.

Constraints and Profits

Obama plans to force improvement in fuel economy by setting a blanket standard for carbon dioxide emissions. That could force less-efficient cars off the market, though the process might take years. The president also has asked Congress to limit greenhouse gas emissions, a move that probably would lead to higher oil prices.

Some economists and environmentalists advocate stiff federal gasoline taxes if the market price does not go high enough on its own; a recent forecast by the federal Energy Information Administration predicted oil prices would double by 2012—but also conceded that the market is so volatile that prices might not go up at all.

Pushing gas prices up could inflict major political damage, particularly if the recession persists. And it could hamper Detroit's recovery in the short term.

"Generally, you don't make private business more profitable by putting on more constraints," said Robert Murphy, an economist at the free-market Institute for Energy Research think tank. If producing more efficient cars is truly the wave of the future, he added, "then why does the government need to force Detroit to do it?"

Periodical Bibliography

The following articles have been selected to supplement the diverse views presented in this chapter.

Marcellus Andrews	"Should We Still Make Things?" *Dissent*, March 11, 2009.
Fred Barnes	"The Other American Auto Industry," *Weekly Standard*, December 22, 2008.
Steve Hargreaves	"Jump-Starting an American Car Town," CNNMoney.com, April 23, 2009.
Daniel J. Ikenson	"Don't Bail Out the Big Three," *American*, November 21, 2008.
Greg Kaza	"Not Our Fathers' Auto Industry," *Chronicles: A Magazine of American Culture*, May 1, 2009.
Tom Krisher	"Why Honda Is Growing as Detroit Falls Behind," *San Francisco Chronicle*, July 3, 2008.
Dan La Botz	"What's to Be Done About the Auto Industry?" *MR Zine*, November 11, 2008.
P.J. O'Rourke	"The End of the Affair," *Wall Street Journal*, May 30, 2009.
Eric Peters	"Too Many Cars, Not Enough Market," *American Spectator*, February 11, 2009.
Jeffrey D. Sachs	"Transforming the Auto Industry," *Scientific American*, February 2009.

OPPOSING
VIEWPOINTS®
SERIES

CHAPTER 4

How Can the United States Meet Its Future Transportation Needs?

Chapter Preface

B etter known as alcohol, ethanol is found in liquor, wine, and beer. However, it makes up about 10 percent of the fuel most Americans pump into their cars. The nation became ethanol's largest producer in 2005, the same year Congress enacted a bill that calls for 8 billion gallons of use by 2012. The United States and Brazil accounted for nearly 90 percent of global ethanol production in 2008; 20 percent of American corn crops are converted into the highly flammable, combustible liquid.

While it has existed for thousands of years, ethanol has been used as a fuel in the nation for at least one hundred years. Henry Ford, the man behind 1908's revolutionary Model T and the Ford Motor Company, proclaimed that ethanol was "the fuel of the future." Ethanol fuel consumption persisted in the following decades, but it was not until the 1970s that it became a potential contender for energy. The Middle East oil embargo against the United States and eventual elimination of lead from gasoline—due to its impact on the environment—led to policies that encouraged the blending of ethanol in fuels.

Amid today's continued reliance on Middle East oil and amplified concerns about global warming, proponents make a vigorous case for ethanol. Says Brian Jennings of the American Coalition for Ethanol, "There is no panacea, no silver bullet solution that will fix our system overnight. But there is one important step already being taken: a growing supply of homegrown, clean-burning, high-performance, renewable fuel that can operate in every single automobile on the road today—ethanol."[1] Opponents, however, argue that ethanol is difficult to transport and that producing ethanol creates destructive emissions and raises food prices. "Using ethanol for energy was supposed to be a win-win situation. . . . But in the real world, unintended consequences are all too frequent,"[2] argues Diana Furchtgott-Roth, a senior fellow at the Hudson Institute. In the following chapter, the authors attempt to predict how America will meet its transportation needs in the near and far future.

Notes

1. *Forbes*, November 16, 2005. www.forbes.com.
2. *American*, April 22, 2008. www.american.com.

> *"It's striking how many solutions public transit promises."*

Public Transportation Is More Efficient

Ryan Avent

Based in Washington, D.C., Ryan Avent is an economic writer and blogger at the Economist's *Free Exchange Blog and Ryan Avent.com. In the following viewpoint, he argues that climbing oil prices, worsening gridlock, and foreboding climate change can be alleviated by public transit. Avent insists that neither electric vehicles nor continued investment in highways will ease traffic congestion or speed up commutes. Green-friendly transit construction, on the other hand, has facilitated encouraging shifts in land use and energy consumption in car-oriented cities at a fraction of the cost, the author says. But Avent believes that public transit is absent from both sides of the transportation debate.*

As you read, consider the following questions:

1. How does Avent support his position that public transit ridership is increasing?

2. How does the author compare budgetary spending on public transit and highways?

3. According to Avent, what are the common perceptions of public transit?

One year ago, as America prepared for the traditional summer-driving crush, op-ed pages nationwide fretted over a disturbing trend. Only a decade earlier, oil had plumbed depths near $10 per barrel, and dirt-cheap gas had allowed us to roll over the nation's blacktop in vehicles of monster-truck proportions. But now something odd was happening: In just nine short years, real oil prices had quadrupled. The steady upward march threatened all that we held dear, like Chevy Tahoes, the open road, and driving alone. How, the nation's pundits wondered in 2007, could America cope with oil at $60 per barrel?

With grim determination, as it turned out. Locked into habits formed over decades of pro-auto policy, motorists doggedly faced down rising prices. Oil has since doubled in price again, and for the most part, the American public continues to motor away. Having busied ourselves building horizontal cities and eight-cylinder engines for decades, we are now woefully unprepared to do otherwise. Better to swallow hard, fill the tank, and hope the whole mess goes away.

But behind our car addiction lies hopeful news. Americans drove 11 billion miles less this March than last March—a 4.3 percent drop, and the steepest one-year reduction since 1942. In 2008, gasoline consumption is on pace to decline for the first time in nearly two decades. And transit ridership is up. Yes, in America.

In 2007, U.S. riders took 10.3 billion trips on transit systems. That marked the highest level in 50 years—since before the Eisenhower interstate system, since a time when streetcars rattled down the boulevards of many American cities. Usage this year is up 3.3 percent nationally over last year's highs.

The largest gains have come, somewhat surprisingly, in predominantly automobile-oriented places like Denver, Dallas, and Charlotte, N.C.

Americans, it seems, are not constitutionally opposed to mass transit. An American public enthralled by automobiles has seen the enemy and [has] begun to look for solutions—to congestion and fuel prices, and to climate change. But those looking have discovered that a half-century of neglect has made travel by transit a challenge.

Seeking options, the nation has found them wanting. The ceaseless climb of oil prices, the growing financial toll of congestion, and the looming cataclysm of global climate change have not yet shaken the men and women entrusted with the care of our infrastructure to act—or moved politicians, the press, and the public to demand action. Why can we not bring ourselves to speak of the need for better transit?

A Token of Our Affection

This failure to speak, to act, represents a huge missed opportunity. Overall, the transportation sector, including cars, is responsible for roughly a third of the nation's energy use and carbon emissions. Department of Energy statistics show that, per passenger-mile, rail transit is substantially greener and less energy-hungry than an automobile—and as transit use increases, systems grow ever more efficient.

Provided that oil markets or government policies continue to pressure drivers, transit demand will grow, and transportation emissions will fall. It's happening already; the shift away from cars slashed emissions by 9 million metric tons in the first three months of 2008.

According to the American Public Transportation Association, American transit use reached its all-time high in 1946, when a population less than half the current size took over 23 billion trips. In the postwar years, riders abandoned transportation systems as government policies fueled suburban growth and a highway boom, and the country's public-transit network fell prey to neglect. The massive migration to sprawl drove ridership downward to a low in 1972 of just 6.5 billion trips.

Today, many commuters cannot easily avoid cranking up the car each morning. Because Americans rely heavily on their cars, reductions in driving have been modest compared to the increase in driving costs. Where transit, walking, or biking aren't options, families must move, change vehicles, or stay home to slow spending—costly and unattractive options for most. Otherwise, higher gas expenditures mean less disposable income.

But energy experts say it's high time for that to change. "Clearly [federal and local governments will] have to make a large new investment in transit and rail," says Joseph Romm, senior fellow at [the Center for] American Progress, calling such investments "inevitable" in response to growing ridership.

Of course, it's important to be realistic: Just under 5 percent of commuters took public transit to work in 2005, and the number likely remains modest despite recent gains. A more comprehensive transit network would be but one small part of a broader package of climate policies. Many transit vehicles continue to use petroleum, leading to a 44 percent increase in transit fuel costs from last year to this year. Electric vehicles are largely spared this pain, but are also only as clean as the fuels generating the power. To truly make transit work, new capacity should be coupled with a cleaner electrical grid.

It's a major undertaking, to be sure. Yet this shouldn't dim our enthusiasm for supporting new transit investments. Today's meager transit funding means that even small budgetary increases could deliver significant results. Annual federal spending on new transit projects is just $1.6 billion—4 percent of the nearly $37 billion allocated to highways.

America can expect to add 150 million people to its population over the next 50 years. This growth will place unprecedented pressure on a transportation network stressed to the breaking point. New high-capacity rail transit within and between cities is necessary to handle this pressure. The American Society of Civil Engineers, which regularly and harshly grades America's crumbling infrastructure, points out that railway investments can be made for "substantially less than the cost of adding equivalent highway capacity," moving more people faster over less mileage. It makes little sense to waste money on low-capacity highways that cater to dirty vehicles in a world where gasoline prices are making driving less attractive by the day.

And in a nation where $78 billion is lost annually to wasted time and fuel as drivers sit on congested roadways, transit offers help. A plug-in automobile in traffic isn't polluting like its internal-combustion neighbors, but it's also not helping its owner get to work faster. Transit can.

In fact, it's striking how many solutions public transit promises. Construction of transit in growing cities like D.C., Denver, and Dallas has facilitated shifts in land-use patterns and increased density. The Brookings Institution's Chris Leinberger argues that rent and home price data suggest substantial interest in walkable urban neighborhoods near transit—places more amenable to reduced driving and energy efficiency than low-density housing. Leinberger estimates that such areas could attract some 30 percent of all new housing demand, slowing exurban sprawl and the resulting "extreme" commutes.

And in a period of economic uncertainty, the idea of employing thousands of Americans to build and operate a new generation of transportation investments should be welcome. The Surface Transportation Policy Project estimates that investments in transit projects generate about 19 percent more jobs than equivalent investments in highway infrastructure.

Wasting 38 Hours per Year

In the "2007 Urban Mobility Report," the Texas Transportation Institute calculates that in 2005 Americans who commuted during peak hours spent an average of 38 hours per year—beyond their normal commutes—in gridlock. Furthermore, the U.S. Transportation secretary has called congestion one of the greatest threats to the nation's economy, noting that drivers annually waste more than four billion hours beyond their normal commutes and about three billion gallons of increasingly costly fuel in traffic jams. The greatest concentration of congestion often occurs along critical transportation corridors, which link residential areas, business centers, sports arenas and shopping areas. Travel demand on U.S. roadways is outpacing available capacity at such a fast rate that new road construction alone will not solve the growing problem.

Michael Baltes, Brian Cronin,
Steve Mortensen, and Dale Thompson,
"Managing Congestion with Integrated Corridor Management,"
Mass Transit, *April-May 2008.*

Transit-oriented development has also proved both green and lucrative for many cities: Metro in Washington, D.C., has helped to attract at least $15 billion in new development. Dallas's younger DART [Dallas Area Rapid Transit] system has so far brought in more than $1 billion in private investments. Other cities have experienced similar successes.

So . . . Why the Silence?

So why are greens and political leaders reluctant to embrace transit as an energy and climate fix? Perception may be a problem. Transit systems are widely seen as dirty, slow, unreliable, and inconvenient relative to automobiles. Romm suggested to me that transit is seen as "not sexy." When folks imagine a greener future, visions of electric cars and solar panels abound. No one thinks of a humble subway car rumbling through dark, century-old tracks beneath Manhattan.

Transit is also widely, and correctly, regarded as disproportionately benefiting the residents of large urban areas and lower income households, and political mathematics are seldom friendly to proposals seen as "urban." Highway money is welcomed anywhere, but transit is considered a highly localized solution. Within metropolitan areas, transit funding often remains controversial, as exurban and highway-dependent jurisdictions feud with leaders from denser areas over the viability of new transit investments.

These conflicts often discourage potential transit champions. As Matthew Yglesias, associate editor at the *Atlantic Monthly* and a frequent commenter on transit and politics, told me in an e-mail, "The biggest obstacle, probably, is that a lot of politicians who should be on the right side of this aren't." He cites Sen. Chuck Schumer (D-N.Y.), who "ought to be leading the charge in the Senate, but instead he's big on opportunistic attacks on the Bush administration for gasoline being too expensive," and Rep. Rahm Emanuel (D-Ill.), who "represents Chicago but doesn't show much leadership on this." As Yglesias puts it, "A lot of politicians from smaller cities or suburbs must be looking at guys like that and saying, 'If *they* don't want to take this on, then I'd really better stay away.'"

And as part of the broader political conversation, transit lingers in relative obscurity. My informal polling of several environmental journalists in Washington suggested that discomfort with available information on transit and emissions reduced their willingness to write on the subject. As such, transit struggles to join the political conversation—and since it's not part of the conversation, writers have little incentive to learn about it. On the cycle goes.

Fortunately, this is changing as interest in climate change grows. New efforts to measure metropolitan carbon footprints illustrate the value of transit as a green technology. A report from Harvard's Kennedy School of Government, published in March by economists Ed Glaeser and Matthew Kahn, notes that even where transit use is highest, "emissions from public transport are a small fraction of per household emissions from private driving. For example, in Chicago and Washington, per household emissions from private cars are more than 10 times the emissions from public transport."

And a new study from the Brookings Institution argues that, "Federal transportation decisions have historically limited the viability of transit and transit-oriented development, which represents an important tool for shrinking carbon footprints by reducing vehicle travel and associated fuel use."

But for all those seeking change, the biggest obstacle to better transit policy has been economic. America enthusiastically built roads and sprawling suburbs for half a century, and for most of that period, gasoline prices dutifully played along. As recently as 1998, as the United States prepared to embark upon a substantial acceleration in its exurban land rush, the *Economist* famously speculated that oil prices might fall from $10 to $2. There was every reason to believe that a life built around driving might be economically sustainable for the foreseeable future.

But of course, the global economy did not cooperate. Exurban sprawl in America led to steady increases in driving and fuel consumption. More important, large nations around the world grew rapidly out of poverty. As their citizens rose from penury, their energy demand increased, placing pressure on an oil supply neglected during the era of cheap oil. The combination of growing demand and stagnating supply did its work. The price of gas is now approaching $4 per gallon nationally, and the economics have changed. It's time for our national conversation to change along with it.

"*Many recent [public] transportation plans produce more congestion and air pollution, not less, and end up wasting people's time, money, and health.*"

Public Transportation Is Not More Efficient

Randal O'Toole

Randal O'Toole is a senior fellow at the Cato Institute and author of The Best-Laid Plans: How Government Planning Harms Your Quality of Life, Your Pocketbook, and Your Future. *In the following excerpt from his book, O'Toole purports that two myths influence transportation planning: Public transit is underfunded and ridership would increase if it were more accessible, and building new roads and freeways cannot ease traffic congestion. He argues that, in reality, costly investments in rail transit are less efficient than buses or freeway-building options and do not stimulate new growth. Yet, under the guise of redeveloping cities and reducing driving, O'Toole maintains that the powerful transit lobbyists work to funnel tax dollars into their pockets.*

Randal O'Toole, *The Best-Laid Plans: How Government Planning Harms Your Quality of Life, Your Pocketbook, and Your Future.* Lynn, MA: Cato Institute, 2007. Copyright © 2007 by Cato Institute. Republished with permission of Cato Institute, conveyed through Copyright Clearance Center, Inc.

As you read, consider the following questions:

1. In O'Toole's view, what groups and parties are represented by the American Public Transportation Association?

2. How did plans in Madison, Wisconsin, to build a commuter rail and improve bus services compare to an alternative to solely enhance the latter, according to O'Toole?

3. In the author's opinion, what creates the impression that new roads and highways lead to more traffic?

Two major myths drive transportation planning in American cities today. First is the assumption that public transit is drastically underfunded and that more people would ride transit if only it were available. "When public policy allows a real choice between the auto and mass transit," writes a professor in the Rutgers University planning school, "a far higher percentage of the population travels by mass transit." Second is the oft-stated claim that "we can't build our way out of congestion."

These myths have led Portland, the San Francisco Bay Area, and many other urban areas to make almost no attempt to relieve congestion by building new roads. Instead, they put most of their transportation funds into expensive transit projects. The result is more congestion and few new transit riders.

Supporting the underfunded-transit myth is the fable urban planners love to tell about how the big bad General Motors (GM) conspired to rid the nation of efficient streetcar systems, supposedly so that people would have to buy GM automobiles and drive rather than take transit. No matter how often researchers at the University of California (Berkeley), University of California (Irvine), Portland State University, and elsewhere have debunked this myth, it continues to persist among rail advocates and auto opponents.

General Motors *was* convicted of conspiring to monopolize the market for buses by having National City Lines, which it partially owned, purchase buses from GM rather than its competitors. But this does not mean it was out to destroy transit systems or that it played a significant role in converting streetcar lines to buses. If anything, GM's infusion of capital into National City Lines may have helped transit systems and transit riders.

As previously noted, transit companies throughout the nation began converting from streetcars to buses as early as 1918, and continued to do so through the 1960s. More than half of the nation's streetcar systems had gone out of business or been replaced by buses long before National City Lines was formed in 1933. From 1933 to 1949, the years during which General Motors is supposed to have carried out its nefarious deeds, more than 300 streetcar systems converted to buses. National City Lines owned or had an interest in fewer than 30 of these systems. In most of the systems, the conversion of streetcars to buses had begun long before National City purchased an interest in the line. National City purchased 12 systems in the very year they converted to buses, suggesting that the decision to convert had been made even before National City got involved.

In 1949, 50 American cities still had streetcars. Although GM divested itself of National City Lines by that year, transit companies (and, in some cases, public transit agencies) continued to convert to buses over the next 17 years. St. Louis was the last to complete its conversion in 1966, leaving just eight U.S. cities with rail transit (including two, Chicago and New York, which converted their streetcar lines to buses in the 1950s but maintained subway, elevated, and commuter rail lines). In short, General Motors was involved, through its partial ownership of National City Lines, in less than 5 percent of the conversions of streetcars to buses.

Transit companies had excellent reasons to convert streetcars to buses: Buses were more flexible and less expensive to buy, cost less to operate, and did not require installation and maintenance of expensive rail and trolley infrastructure. "The faithful electric trolley had sunk into such a state of obsolescence as to be scarcely tolerable," *Fortune* magazine wrote in 1936. The new buses were popular among transit riders: When New York streetcar companies replaced trolleys with buses, ridership increased by as much as 50 to 60 percent. GM took advantage of this transition to sell more of its buses, but the transition would have taken place with or without GM's involvement. "Buses were clearly a better way to go and would have taken over with or without GM," says University of Arizona transportation researcher Sandra Rosenbloom.

The General Motors conspiracy myth is popular because it supports the larger myth that a powerful highway lobby promoted huge subsidies to highways and auto driving, leaving the transit industry unable to compete. This myth is used to justify increased subsidies to transit today, with an emphasis on rail transit to undo the damage supposedly caused by the GM conspiracy.

The Transit Lobby

Although autos and oil are two of the largest industries in America, auto manufacturers and oil companies barely lifted a finger in support of the Interstate Highway Act of 1956 [officially known as the Federal-Aid Highway Act of 1956] or any federal or state highway legislation since. Instead, most lobbying has come from truckers and construction companies. But most construction companies can profit equally from building rail lines as building highways, so the notion of an all-powerful highway lobby is a myth. In fact, what remains of a highway lobby has been losing ground to an increasingly powerful transit lobby since 1981, when Congress first diverted highway user fees to transit. The transit lobby has been dominant at least since 1991, when Congress directed cities to undertake comprehensive transportation planning that, in many cases, favored transit funding over highways.

The transit lobby is represented by the American Public Transportation Association, whose membership includes

- close to 400 U.S. transit agencies;

- more than 70 other government agencies, such as regional councils of governments and state departments of transportation;

- nearly 400 engineering and consulting firms;

- more than 450 manufacturers and suppliers;

- 20 companies that manage transit services for public transit agencies;

- 7 contractors and land developers; and

- more than 70 quasi-governmental and nonprofit organizations.

Collectively, the U.S. transit industry spent more than $40 billion in 2004. Since more than three-quarters of that comes from taxpayers, the various agencies and companies within the industry have a huge incentive to lobby Congress and state and local governments. A typical transit-planning program may work as follows.

First, the regional transit agency and local governments form a *transportation management association*. Normally, state laws prevent local governments from lobbying taxpayers, but the transportation management association offers a way around this. The association accepts money from private companies, such as potential rail contractors, as well as tax dollars from the transit agency and local governments. The association uses some of this money to conduct "public involvement processes," which are really little more than propaganda exercises in favor of increased transit funding.

The association or the transit agency itself will also hire a consultant such as Parsons Brinckerhoff to study transit alternatives in the region or one corridor in the region. Parsons Brinckerhoff built New York City's first subway line and since then has probably been involved in one way or another in a majority of U.S. rail transit projects. The company knows that if it recommends that a rail line be built, it is likely to get the contract to engineer the project, so it has a strong incentive to slant the analysis toward rail. This does not mean that the consultant will "cook the books," only that it will find justifications for building rail even when other alternatives would make more sense.

A Crippled Alternative

A transportation management association in Madison, Wisconsin, hired Parsons Brinckerhoff to analyze a rail transit proposal. The company compared several alternatives. If Madison continued to grow but did nothing to improve its bus system, the consultant estimated buses would carry 12.4 million passengers a year by 2020. But if Madison spent $60 million "enhancing" its bus system, it would carry more than 18.8 million passengers in 2020. The cost of each new rider (using the Federal Transit Administration formula) would be about $1.50, much of which would be offset by fares.

Next, Parsons Brinckerhoff prepared an alternative that included both the bus enhancements plus one new commuter rail line costing $180 million, or three times as much as all the bus enhancements. To its disappointment, the company's computer models projected that this alternative would actually carry *fewer* riders than the bus enhancements alone. So the consulting firm crippled the enhanced bus alternative by "deleting duplicative service and the least-productive routes." The crippled bus alternative was projected to carry 18.5 million riders in 2020, or 0.3 million less than the rail alternative. Even if these numbers were valid, the 0.3 million additional rail riders would cost an average of $65 apiece—more than 40 times as much as new riders under the enhanced bus alternative.

At least Parsons Brinckerhoff was honest enough to admit that this is how it prepared the alternatives. The transportation management association was not so candid. When presenting the alternatives to the public, they not only deleted the enhanced bus alternative, they deleted the crippled-enhanced alternative. That left only the do-nothing alternative and rail, making it appear that rail transit was needed to increase ridership from 12.4 to 18.8 million trips per year. . . .

Political Support from Landowners

Rail transit also influences property values in parts of an urban region, and that leads to political support from the landowners who benefit. Contrary to frequent claims, rail transit does not stimulate new investment in a region. An analysis by University of California planning professor Robert Cervero and Parsons Brinckerhoff consultant Samuel Seskin found that "urban rail transit investments rarely 'create' new growth." However, they added, rail investments may "redistribute growth that would have taken place without the investment." The main redistribution was from the suburbs to downtown, which explains why downtown property owners tend to strongly support rail transit projects.

While rail transit does not by itself stimulate new investments, the Federal Transit Administration has required most cities that have built rail transit to attempt to boost ridership by promoting transit-oriented developments. Many if not most of these developments are supported by tax-increment financing, tax breaks, or other subsidies. This has spawned a new industry of realtors and developers who thrive on tax subsidies to high-density developments.

Portland claims that its streetcar line has generated $2.3 billion worth of development. What it fails to mention is that the streetcar line passes through three urban-renewal districts, and that the city has spent more than two-thirds of a billion dollars subsidizing the redevelopment of those districts.

Between the transit bureaucracies, consulting firms, contractors, developers, and other special interest groups, the one interest group that is often forgotten is the group for which transit ostensibly exists: transit riders. Curiously, few if any members of the American Public Transportation Association truly represent this group. Even the "public interest groups" that the association counts among its members are mostly special interests such as the Concrete Reinforcing Steel Institute and the National Railroad Construction and Maintenance Association.

Transit riders themselves divide into two groups: transit-dependent people who cannot drive and transit-choice people who can drive but prefer to ride transit. Normally, both groups tend to settle in cities that have intensive transit service rather than in the suburbs. Rail transit, and most transit planning, seems to be aimed at expanding the second market by attracting suburbanites out of their cars. Since rail transit so often ends up sacrificing bus services to or raising fares for transit-dependent people, it would seem to make much more sense instead to increase bus services in the cities and corridors where most people who prefer or depend on transit already reside. But planners, bedazzled by the mantra of "transportation choices," have focused instead on rails: In addition to the 25 urban areas that had rail transit in 2004, at least three dozen more cities are planning or proposing rail projects.

In supporting rail transit, urban planners allowed themselves to become tools of powerful special interests whose main goal is to transfer dollars from taxpayers to their own pockets. Planners justify this by the need to "redevelop" cities to reduce auto driving. But the hard cold truth is that rail

Light Rail's Real Impact on Traffic

The claim is that [light rail] will lure drivers out of their cars and, thereby, reduce traffic congestion. If all of the light rail passengers would have otherwise been driving their own cars, light rail would, on average, be removing three cars in 1,000 from the roads. However, studies have shown that about 80% of new light rail passengers were former bus passengers. Taking this into account, the real impact on traffic is for light rail to remove less than one car in 1,000 from traffic.

John Semmens,
"Public Transit: A Bad Product at a Bad Price,"
WebMemo, *#213, Heritage Foundation, February 13, 2003.*

transit does little to shape cities, especially when it so often actually reduces transit ridership. At most, it offers planners an excuse to rezone neighborhoods to higher densities.

The Induced-Demand Myth

If rail transit cannot significantly relieve congestion, is there an alternative that can? Or are we doomed to be "stuck in traffic," as Brookings Institution economist Anthony Downs named his book about congestion problems? The answer is that we *can* build our way out of congestion if new construction is combined with better road pricing.

Downs points out that people respond to congestion in one of several ways. Some may simply suffer through it, but others change their times of travel or travel routes. A few switch to public transit or other modes, and some may not travel at all. When a new highway opens, or a highway's capacity is increased, people respond by switching back to the times or routes that were most convenient to them. This creates the impression that new roads are just as congested as the old ones and fuels the claim that new roads simply "induce" more traffic.

The induced-demand myth—the claim that it is pointless to build new highways because they merely increase driving—is especially peculiar because it is so irrational. It is the dream of every private entrepreneur to find a product so desirable that people will consume more the more it is made. Only the government would be criticized for building things that people use and urged instead to build things, such as rail transit lines, that receive little use.

If it were really true that new freeways merely induce more traffic, then the interstate freeways of Sioux Falls, South Dakota, or Cheyenne, Wyoming, would be just as congested as the freeways of Los Angeles or San Francisco. Of course, they are not. Instead of speaking of "induced demand," it would be more accurate to describe such demand as "suppressed demand" that is relieved by new roads. Even University of California planning professor Robert Cervero admits that most induced-driving studies "have suffered from methodological problems" and that "wrongheaded . . . claims of induced demand have stopped highway projects in their tracks."

The Tampa-Hillsborough [County] Expressway Authority recently completed an innovative new highway that proves cities can build their way out of congestion. The authority manages an east-west tollway through Tampa, part of which was congested at near-gridlock levels during morning and evening rush hours. The authority knew that three-fourths of its morning traffic moved in the direction of downtown Tampa and three-fourths of the afternoon traffic moved in the opposite direction.

Without buying any significant new right of way, the authority built three new lanes that it uses for inbound traffic in the morning and outbound traffic in the afternoon. For a considerable portion of the highway, the new lanes were elevated above the existing road and built on piers that occupy just six feet in the median strip of the existing highway. Since the authority effectively has six new lanes—three inbound and three outbound—it says it built six lanes in six feet.

The new elevated lanes were expected to cost a total of $7 million per lane mile, but turned out to cost twice that due to an engineering error made by a consultant hired by the authority. Even $14 million per lane mile is less than a third of the cost per mile of the average light-rail line that is currently proposed or under construction. Moreover, 100 percent of the elevated expressway cost is being paid for by tolls; the road cost taxpayers nothing. The new lanes are electronically tolled; people who buy a transponder pay $1.50 every time they use it; the authority photographs the license plates of cars without transponders and sends them a bill for $1.75.

Since the lanes first opened in July 2006, congestion on both the new and existing lanes dropped from level of service F, meaning near-gridlock or stop-and-go traffic, to level of service B, meaning traffic moves at a "reasonably free flow." If congestion increases, the authority plans to use value-priced tolls—tolls that increase during heavy traffic periods—to ensure that the new lanes are never congested. This means that the local transit agency can put express buses on such lanes and those buses can move as fast or faster than any rail line.

The new, elevated express lanes did not result from the long-range transportation planning that has been required by federal law since 1991. In fact, it would be more accurate to say that the lanes were built in spite of such planning. Instead of express lanes, the Hillsborough County Metropolitan Planning Organization had written a light-rail line into its plans. This line would have required huge tax subsidies and done little or nothing to relieve traffic congestion. Fortunately for Tampa commuters, the Tampa-Hillsborough [County] Expressway Authority is funded out of tolls, not federal tax dollars, so it could build the lanes regardless of the planners' wishes.

One lesson here is that the solution to congestion has as much to do with institutional design as with infrastructure. Many of the cities that are doing the most to relieve congestion are doing so with independent toll road authorities that are funded out of user fees. Such authorities have an incentive to relieve congestion because such relief increases their revenues. . . .

On the Horizon

Other low-cost solutions to congestion are also on the horizon. A considerable amount of congestion is caused by drivers' slow reaction times. In heavy traffic, one car slowing down can create a wave of slower traffic that can take hours to work itself out. Improving reaction speeds can eliminate such waves. Some new cars today have *adaptive cruise control*, also known as laser-guide cruise control, which allows the car to instantly respond to changes in speed of the car before it. Traffic engineers at the University of Minnesota estimate that, when 20 percent of cars on the road have adaptive cruise control—which is expected by 2010—much of this congestion will disappear. In effect, adaptive cruise control increases roadway capacities without building any new roads.

An even longer-term solution to congestion will come in the form of intelligent highways that are wired to control vehicles. Some state highway agencies are already placing wires in roads capable of sending signals to vehicles. Meanwhile, automakers are introducing cars that can accelerate, brake, and steer themselves. It would be a simple matter to put a receiver in the car that can get signals from the roads. Since computer-controlled cars could safely drive within a few feet of one another, this system could triple road capacities. Such systems should be available by about 2020.

Until such systems are operating, more highway capacity will be needed in the nation's most congested cities. If built with public-private partnerships and funded out of tolls, such capacity may not require any taxpayer subsidies. If built as elevated roads similar to the Tampa expressway, road capacities can be increased with minimal purchases for new rights of way. Such capacity increases can save people time and money while reducing air pollution and fuel consumption. One of the main obstacles to such solutions to congestion is the urban planning process that gives undue influence to the minority of people who oppose the automobile.

Urban planners promised to provide balanced transportation planning that considered a wide range of social benefits and costs. Instead, they focused on extremely narrow concerns: promoting downtown property owners over suburban property owners; promoting rail construction over road construction; and creating auto-hostile environments. Planners assumed that anything that might reduce driving was good, no matter what the cost to auto users or society in general. Even if reducing driving is a good thing, planners rarely asked whether their tools—more congestion and more money spent on rail transit and other non-road projects—would actually reduce driving. In fact, many recent transportation plans produce more congestion and air pollution, not less, and end up wasting people's time, money, and health.

> "By using innovative and cost-effective technology to increase our fuel economy, we can protect the environment, create jobs, and make America safer and more secure."

Fuel-Efficiency Standards Should Be Raised

Sierra Club

In the following viewpoint, the Sierra Club advocates raising the corporate average fuel economy (CAFE) of cars, pickup trucks, and sport utility vehicles (SUVs). The group alleges that vehicles nationally account for 80 percent of oil consumption and 20 percent of carbon dioxide emissions. Therefore, it maintains that CAFE be increased to an average of forty miles per gallon (MPG), which would save 3 million barrels of oil a day and cut emissions by 600 million tons a year. Innovative technologies to achieve higher efficiency standards with safety are in reach, the group continues, and loopholes to foregoing them must be closed. Founded in 1892, the Sierra Club is the nation's oldest environmental organization.

As you read, consider the following questions:

1. As stated by the Sierra Club, how can fuel economy be raised for SUVs?

2. How does the group support its statement that improving fuel economy will create domestic jobs?

3. Why must fuel-economy tests be reevaluated, in the group's view?

By making our cars, pickup trucks, and SUVs [sport utility vehicles] go farther on a gallon of gas, Americans can save billions of dollars, curb global warming pollution, and slash our dependence on oil—making our nation safer and more secure. In 1975, Congress enacted corporate average fuel economy (CAFE) standards, doubling the fuel economy of new vehicles. By enacting these standards, the United States saves approximately 3 million barrels of oil per day, making it the most successful energy-saving measure ever adopted. However, despite breakthroughs in gas-saving technology, the government has allowed fuel economy standards to stagnate and auto companies have hawked inefficient SUVs and other trucks for nearly 20 years. As a result, the fuel economy of today's new vehicles has fallen to the lowest level in over two decades. It doesn't have to be this way. By using innovative and cost-effective technology to increase our fuel economy, we can protect the environment, create jobs, and make America safer and more secure.

Cars and light trucks account for 40% of U.S. oil consumption and emit 20% of the nation's carbon dioxide (CO_2) pollution, the heat-trapping gas that causes global warming. Because each gallon of gasoline burned pumps 28 pounds of CO_2 into the atmosphere, the average car emits about 63 tons of CO_2 over its lifetime—and the average SUV or pickup emits around 82 tons. In comparison: America's automobiles produce more global warming pollution than all the vehicles, power plants, and factories in Great Britain combined.

If all of the vehicles in the United States averaged 40 miles per gallon (mpg) we would save over 3 million barrels of oil each day; that is more oil than the United States currently imports from the Persian Gulf and could ever extract from the Arctic National Wildlife Refuge, combined. Getting 40 mpg would cut global warming pollution by 600 million tons a year and save consumers more than $45 billion each year at the gas pump. The United States is the world's largest global warming polluter—we must take the lead in reducing this pollution.

Innovative Technology Can Help Free Us from Our Oil Dependence

Modern technology is the key to increasing fuel economy and saving oil. Between 1975 and the late 1980s, better engines, transmissions, materials, and aerodynamics accounted for 86% of fuel economy improvements. Existing fuel-saving technology can raise fuel economy even further. In 2002, the National Academy of Sciences found that with current technology we could "significantly reduce fuel consumption within 15 years."

The technology exists to make all new vehicles—from cars to SUVs to pickup trucks—go farther on a gallon of gas. These fuel-saving technologies are on the road today in some vehicles, but should be in all. A 2003 study by the Union of Concerned Scientists [UCS] titled "Building a Better SUV" analyzed the fuel economy benefits of many of these technologies.

- Advanced Ignitions: By replacing a conventional starter-motor and alternator with an Integrated Starter Generator (ISG), a gas engine can switch off when the vehicle is stopped and idling. Vehicles burn as much as

15% of their gas while sitting in traffic. The ISG restarts the motor when you put your foot on the gas, just like tapping a computer mouse to awaken a sleeping computer, and saves added fuel by doing it more efficiently than a standard starter. Fuel Economy Improvement: 15–25%

- High Strength, Lightweight Materials: Strong, lightweight steel, aluminum, and plastics can all play a role in helping vehicles shed weight while enhancing safety. Fuel Economy Improvement: 25–30%

- Sleeker Design: Improving the aerodynamics cuts down on wind resistance and installing low rolling resistance tires reduces road friction. Fuel Economy Improvement: 5%

- Smarter Transmissions: A Continuously Variable Transmission (CVT) allows for an infinite number of gear ratios for the most efficient combination of engine speed and wheel speed. With a CVT, gears are replaced by continuous belts to maximize efficiency. A 2001 study by the trade publication *Automotive News* estimated a 20% fuel economy gain from a CVT.

- High-Tech Engines: By allowing engine intake valves to close early during low demand, variable valve timing prevents inefficient pumping. Adding lean-burn technology, which introduces more air to the combustion chamber, can provide further efficiency. Fuel economy gains also occur when engines have four valves per cylinder instead of two, individual cylinder control, and cylinder deactivation, which improve fuel economy by automatically shutting down unneeded cylinders when less power is required. *Automotive News* found that cylinder deactivation alone would result in as much as a 20% improvement in fuel economy.

We Can Safely Improve Our Fuel Economy

Long-time safety advocates, such as the Center for Auto Safety, support increasing CAFE standards to 40 miles per gallon— and point out that we can do so safely. A joint study by the Union of Concerned Scientists and the Center for Auto Safety found that raising the fuel economy of new cars and light trucks to 40 mpg would benefit "consumers, the economy and the environment without sacrificing passenger safety."

In fact, the rate of traffic fatalities fell 50% during the same period fuel economy doubled due to CAFE standards. Auto manufacturers claim they can only achieve higher CAFE standards by changing their entire fleets to smaller cars. But they said the same thing in 1974 when a Ford spokesperson testified before Congress that a 27.5 mpg standard would result in a "Ford product line consisting of either all Pinto-sized vehicles or some mix of vehicles ranging from a sub-sub-compact to perhaps a Maverick." Obviously, they were wrong then—and they are wrong again today.

Hybrids—Evolving to Cleaner Cars. Hybrid vehicles are already turning heads and generating excitement. Hybrid vehicles combine an efficient gasoline engine with an electric motor to get great fuel economy. The two engines work in tandem to provide power and speed. When hybrids brake, they recharge the batteries using energy that other cars just waste. This process is known as regenerative braking. And since both the gasoline engine and the regenerative braking charge the electric motor, hybrid vehicles never need to be plugged in! You just fill them up at the gas station like any other car—only not as often. Hybrid technology can help make automakers' fleets average 40 miles per gallon within the next ten years.

A hybrid exists to fit the needs of almost any driver. There are already several models of hybrids on the road today— from the two-seater Honda Insight, to the 5 passenger Honda

True Fuel Efficiency Drifting from Reality

For better or worse, hybrids have become the poster child for vehicles not living up to fuel economy expectations. That may be because hybrid drivers are theoretically more interested in saving oil and thus complain louder; because hybrids display real-time mpg [miles per gallon] results and thus their drivers are more aware of the results; or perhaps simply because, as the reigning mpg champ, they're an easy target.

The truth, however, is that advertised fuel economies of *all* vehicles, including conventional models, have been slowly but steadily drifting from reality for more than two decades.

James Kliesch,
"Gas Mileage: Why MPG Numbers Really Matter,"
Mother Earth News, *August-September 2007.*

Civic Sedan and Toyota Prius hatchback, to the Ford Escape hybrid SUV. The next few years will see a surge of hybrid vehicles into the market, giving consumers more choices and greater opportunities to reduce our dependence on oil, slash global warming pollution, and save money at the pump. Continued advances in hybrid technology will improve fuel economy and lower vehicle costs. Additionally, hybrid technology is ready to make its appearance in the largest SUVs, vans, and pickup trucks.

With Innovative Technology, Even SUVs Can Get Great Fuel Economy. Using existing fuel-saving technology, automakers can improve the fuel economy of any car, pickup truck or SUV. Sadly, this technology is sitting on the shelf because a loophole in the law holds SUVs, pickups and other light trucks to a weaker miles-per-gallon standard than cars. Since light trucks now account for over half of all new vehicles sold, this loophole means that billions of gallons of gasoline are needlessly burned each year, emitting millions of tons of global warming pollution into the atmosphere. But SUV owners should also be able to get great fuel economy. In 2004, Ford Motor Company unveiled the Hybrid Escape, an SUV that gets 33 mpg. Most auto manufacturers are now set to build hybrid versions of pickup trucks and large SUVs, proving that a big vehicle doesn't have to waste a lot of gas.

Creating Clean Cars in America Creates Jobs at Home

The Union of Concerned Scientists' recent study showed that higher fuel economy in cars and light trucks will create jobs throughout the economy. UCS estimates that the auto industry alone will gain 40,000 new jobs. In addition, the money consumers save at the gas pump will be reinvested in the economy, creating an estimated additional 161,000 net new jobs nationwide.

Requiring auto companies to build cleaner cars will make automakers more competitive. The Big Three put auto industry jobs at risk by failing to use innovative technology. While Japanese and European carmakers are putting lean-burn engines, continuously variable transmissions, and other fuel-efficient technologies into their cars, American automakers continue to produce inefficient designs with primitive technology. Already dozens of unionized factories in the United States produce clean car technology. We could do even more by putting American ingenuity to work to make clean, efficient, American-made cars and SUVs.

Making a Great Law Even Better

CAFE has been highly successful in cutting pollution and reducing our oil consumption, but changes in the auto market have taken advantage of weaknesses in the CAFE system. In addition to raising CAFE standards to 40 miles per gallon, the CAFE program should be updated to reflect current trends in driving and the automotive industry.

- Truth in Testing—The fuel economy test administered by EPA [Environmental Protection Agency] does not reflect current driving conditions. It exaggerates the fuel economy of tested vehicles 17–20% by assuming people spend less time driving in congested cities than they actually do. By revising CAFE tests, we could more accurately measure the actual fuel economy of cars and light trucks.

- Close the SUV Loophole—CAFE standards hold SUVs and light trucks to weaker standards than cars. Cars, SUVs, pickup trucks, and vans are all used to carry passengers and can all benefit from modern fuel-efficient technology. By closing this loophole, the United States would save one million barrels of oil a day and reduce our oil dependence.

- Close the "Flexible Fuel Vehicle" Loophole—To encourage the use of alternative fuels—like ethanol—automakers receive credit toward meeting CAFE standards when they build vehicles that can run on them. Unfortunately, these vehicles rarely, if ever, take advantage of their "flexible fuel" ability. According to the Department of Transportation, in 2000 less than 1% of the 1.2 million flexible fuel vehicles on the road actually ran on ethanol.

Driving Us Backward

Despite having the technology to build the fuel-efficient technologies we need, opponents of CAFE in the government and the auto industry are working to weaken this law. Here are a few examples of their recent efforts:

- Creating Perverse Incentives—Weight-based standards categorize vehicles based on their weight and allow heavier vehicles to meet weaker standards. This system would create an incentive for automakers to add weight to their vehicles to qualify them for more relaxed standards. Auto companies already add weight to SUVs and other trucks like the HUMMER, Dodge Ram 2500, and Excursion to exempt these vehicles from CAFE standards.

- Manipulating the System—Opponents of CAFE have also proposed a system that would allow auto manufacturers to trade fuel economy credits between companies. This system would undermine efforts to raise the fuel economy for the entire fleet of vehicles, and provide more opportunities for auto manufacturers to build gas-guzzlers.

> *"Experience with CAFE [corporate average fuel economy] and other government efficiency standards demonstrates that these programs have often produced disastrous results."*

Fuel-Efficiency Standards Harm Americans

Sam Kazman

Sam Kazman is general counsel at the Competitive Enterprise Institute (CEI), a nonprofit organization for public policy in Washington DC. In the following viewpoint, Kazman proclaims that raising corporate average fuel economy (CAFE) will harm motorists in several ways. In his opinion, increasing fuel-efficiency standards hinders consumer choice, creates higher vehicle prices, and counteracts the conservation effects of escalating oil costs. Most of all, Kazan argues that CAFE results in more dangerous roads: Downsizing the production of vehicles to smaller, lighter, more fuel-efficient models compromises driver and passenger safety.

As you read, consider the following questions:

1. How does the author explain the link between vehicle size and safety?

2. What example does Kazman use to support his allegation that efficiency standards can undermine technology?

3. As described by Kazman, what occurred with the use of fuel-efficiency tires?

Invoking global warming and high gasoline prices, politicians are on an energy-efficiency kick. Numerous proposals to boost efficiency standards for a huge array of items—from furnaces to appliances to cars—are on the table. The Senate may soon take up one of the most prominent of these, the Renewable Fuels, Consumer Protection, and Energy Efficiency Act of 2007 (S. 1419).

In the case of automotive standards—known as CAFE, for corporate average fuel economy—the controversy involves not whether to raise the standards, but by how much. The debate sounds like a political poker game. "27.5 mpg is too low; let's raise it to 30." "I'll see your 30 and raise it to 35." "I'll match your 35 and throw in light trucks."

But experience with CAFE and other government efficiency standards demonstrates that these programs have often produced disastrous results. For these reasons, Congress should focus its attention not on making these standards more stringent, but on scrapping them. At a minimum, it should avoid making them worse.

CAFE has many things wrong with it. It raises new car prices, forcing some consumers, especially those with low incomes, to hold on longer to their old cars. It restricts consumer choice, since manufacturers are forced to pay more attention to what the law requires rather than to what consumers want. It is highly questionable at a time of rising gas prices. And worst of all is CAFE's lethal impact on auto safety. When these are taken into account, the case for making this program even more stringent falls apart entirely.

CAFE Kills

CAFE restricts the production of larger, heavier vehicles. These vehicles are lower in fuel economy, but they are also safer than similarly equipped smaller cars. For this reason, while CAFE may improve fuel economy, it also increases traffic deaths.

The relationship between vehicle size and safety is well established. Larger cars have more mass to absorb crash forces, and more interior space in which their occupants can "ride down" a collision before striking a dashboard or side pillar. The smallest cars have occupant death rates that are more than twice those of large cars.

CAFE's trade-off of safety for fuel economy is widely documented. A 2002 National Academy of Sciences study concluded that CAFE's downsizing effect contributed to between 1,300 and 2,600 deaths in a single representative year, and to 10 times that many serious injuries. A 1989 Brookings-Harvard study estimated that CAFE caused a 14 to 27 percent increase in occupant fatalities—an annual toll of 2,200 to 3,900 deaths. A 1999 *USA Today* analysis concluded that, over its lifetime, CAFE had resulted in 46,000 additional fatalities.

CAFE's advocates frequently deny that CAFE has any adverse safety effect at all. Safety advocates such as the Center for Auto Safety and Ralph Nader support increasing CAFE to 45 mpg and contend, in the Sierra Club's words, that "we can do so safely."

But Nader took a totally different view years ago, when large cars weren't as politically incorrect as they are now. In a 1989 interview on what type of car he'd buy, Nader said, "Well, larger cars are safer—there is more bulk to protect the occupant. But they are less fuel-efficient." Asked which cars are least safe, he replied: "The tiny ones." The Center for Auto

Safety took the same position. In 1972 it published a detailed critique of the Volkswagen Beetle, *Small on Safety: The Designed-In Dangers of the Volkswagen*, which explained how "small size and light weight impose inherent limitations" on safety. In short, CAFE has a lethal impact, regardless of what its advocates say today.

New Technologies Will Not Eliminate CAFE's Lethal Effects

Advocates of higher CAFE standards argue that while the program may have reduced vehicle safety in the past, new technologies allow us to escape this trade-off in the future. They point to the fact that cars can be made more fuel-efficient in ways that don't involve downsizing.

Such technologies certainly exist—hybrid engines, improved aerodynamics, and advanced transmissions are examples. But stringent CAFE standards will restrict vehicle weight regardless. No matter what fuel-saving technologies we put into the car of the future, adding weight to that car will both lower its fuel efficiency and increase its safety. A large hybrid sedan, for example, will be safer than a similar small hybrid sedan.

As safety researcher Dr. Leonard Evans, former president of the International Traffic Medicine Association, points out, the no-trade-off argument is like "a tobacco executive claiming that smoking isn't risky because exercise and good diet can make smokers healthier." No matter how fit you are, there is always a trade-off between smoking and health. No matter how advanced automotive technology might become, there will still be a trade-off between fuel economy and safety.

Efficiency Standards Can Unexpectedly Ruin Even Simple Technologies

According to the June 2007 issue of *Consumer Reports*, the cleaning ability of affordable top-loading washers has been ruined by federal energy efficiency rules. The magazine noted:

More Efficient and Less Intrusive

Rather than regulating automobile size, a switch from income to energy taxes might be the most efficient and least intrusive way to reduce consumption and encourage new technology, thereby allowing consumers who want large vehicles and warm houses to have them.

Given the nature of our political system, income taxes will never get replaced by energy taxes. Just as politicians are now set to raise taxes in 2010, they will always be tempted to layer new taxes on top of old, increasing inefficiency and slowing economic growth.

Diana Furchtgott-Roth,
"Skip This CAFE,"
New York Sun, *May 25, 2007.*

"Not so long ago you could count on most washers to get your clothes very clean. Not anymore . . . What happened? As of January, the U.S. Department of Energy has required washers to use 21 percent less energy, a goal we wholeheartedly support. But our tests have found that traditional top-loaders . . . are having a tough time wringing out those savings without sacrificing cleaning ability, the main reason you buy a washer."

It concluded: "[F]or the first time in years we can't call any washer a Best Buy because models that did a very good job getting laundry clean cost $1,000 or more." This is a far cry from the agency's claim that the rule would not affect cleaning ability. If government efficiency standards can ruin something as simple as a washing machine, who knows what they will do to far more complex technologies like cars?

If Energy-Saving Technologies Work, They Don't Need Laws Mandating Their Use

Government higher efficiency mandates are often accompanied by admissions that they may raise prices. But, their advocates claim, those higher prices will be more than offset by reduced operating costs, leaving consumers on balance better off.

These claims are impossible to verify in advance. As the washing machine fiasco demonstrates, it's often impossible to know just how a new technology will work out in practice. But what is clear is that forcing such technologies on the public strongly indicates that the claims being made for them are suspect. After all, if these new technologies are so good, then why do we need laws forcing consumers to buy them?

Higher CAFE Standards Will Undermine the Conservation Effect of High Gasoline Prices

The post-Katrina [Hurricane Katrina] gas price increases have significantly altered Americans' car-buying patterns. Hybrids have grown in popularity. Large SUVs [sport utility vehicles] have dropped in sales while smaller, more fuel-efficient crossover models have gained customers. This May [2007], for [the] first time in five years, passenger car sales exceeded light truck and SUV sales.

But making CAFE more stringent would reduce this consumer response. Fuel economy mandates make driving less expensive on a per-mile basis, encouraging both more driving and less attention to gas prices. One of the great ironies of the CAFE debate is that those who decry our alleged "addiction to cheap oil" are often at the forefront of making oil even cheaper, in terms of cost per mile driven, by promoting higher CAFE standards.

Fuel-Saving Technologies That Look Great on Paper Can Be Risky in Practice

The Union of Concerned Scientists (UCS), a leading advocate of higher CAFE standards, touts its portfolio of "blueprints" for more fuel-efficient vehicles. According to UCS, these blueprints feature existing technologies that automakers can readily utilize; presumably, only industry stubbornness prevents us from having these vehicles.

Yet things are not that simple. Consider the fuel-efficient tires that UCS advocates. Several years ago, Ford attempted to use such tires for its Explorer, and the results were disastrous. Scores of people died as a result of blowouts in defective Firestone tires. A 2001 report by UCS's colleagues at Public Citizen made clear that the quest for higher fuel economy lay behind this episode. According to the report, Ford had first asked that the recommended inflation pressure for the Explorer tires be lowered to reduce rollover risk. That, however, raised the tires' rolling resistance and worsened the vehicle's fuel efficiency. To compensate, Ford then asked Firestone to design a lighter tire. That is when the trouble began.

The connection between the Ford-Firestone issue and fuel economy was rarely raised in the press. Both Public Citizen and UCS continue to advocate higher CAFE standards, acting as if this episode never occurred.

CAFE may well be one of the worst regulatory programs ever. It restricts consumer choice, raises new vehicle prices, and undercuts the price signals that lead people to conserve gasoline. Most importantly, it kills—a fact its advocates have rarely acknowledged. Despite this, CAFE may well be made even more stringent. For the reasons discussed above, that would be an immensely unfortunate result.

Fuel economy mandates are a highly questionable form of regulation that deserve to be reexamined, and CAFE is the best place to start.

| *"America's auto fleet is hardly green, but it's getting greener."*

Green Cars Can Help the United States Meet Its Transportation Needs

Jim Motavalli

Jim Motavalli announces the arrival of greener, cleaner cars in the following viewpoint. The automobile industry, according to him, is flourishing with fuel-efficient and alternative energy research and development. For instance, Motavalli claims that General Motors' upcoming Chevrolet Volt will take the renowned gas-electric hybrid to the next level. Also, he proposes that advances are being made in high-mileage diesel, solving its primary drawback as a high-emissions fuel. Motavalli further contends that the clean-burning fuel cell, which coverts hydrogen to electricity, may one day succeed the internal combustion engine. The author is editor of E—The Environmental Magazine.

As you read, consider the following questions:

1. How does Motavalli answer to the concern that plug-in hybrids consume electricity from coal-burning sources?

2. What is the main advantage of Partial Zero Emission Vehicles (PZEV), as described by Motavalli?

3. What breakthroughs show the potential of all-electric battery engines, according to the author?

The verdict is in on hybrid cars: Americans love them. But just suppose, some environmentalists have been asking, you had a bigger battery pack in your hybrid and the ability to plug it into the wall. Wouldn't that give you the ability to drive to work on electric power, with the small gas engine available in reserve for longer trips? This concept started out as an environmentalist's dream, propelled by activists like Felix Kramer of CalCars.org and the utility-backed Plug-In Partners. But now it's headed for the market. And other high-tech green cars are on their way, too.

In 2005, the late Dave Hermance, then Toyota's environmental engineering guru, had this to say about plug-in hybrid vehicles: "At some point it might be feasible, but it isn't there yet." He added, "They say this is the next great thing, but it just isn't."

What a difference a year makes. In 2006, Toyota was singing a rather different tune. The plug-in hybrid, Hermance said in an interview, "is an appealing technology in terms of energy diversity for transportation. Depending on the grid mix, it may offer reduced life cycle carbon dioxide (CO_2) and reduce fuel consumption at the same time." Others go further. Dr. Andrew Frank, a mechanical engineering professor at the University of California, Davis, envisions a plug-in hybrid that can achieve 60 miles of all-electric range using a currently available, 350-pound lithium-ion battery pack that would last 150,000 miles.

A New Day for Clean Cars

Interest in cleaner and greener auto technology is exploding. From fuel cells to plug-in hybrids, the industry is showing more research and development zeal than at any time since the halcyon days of 1900, when gasoline, steam and electric vehicles (EVs) were competing in the marketplace. Companies such as General Motors [GM], ridiculed for stodginess and worse in films like *Roger & Me* and *Who Killed the Electric Car?* are revealing a much leaner side. In fact, GM has made the first plug-in hybrid production commitment in the United States, using an intriguing new approach. It is developing an entirely new propulsion system, shown at the recent Detroit Auto Show as the Chevrolet Volt.

The new GM car is not a standard parallel hybrid like the Toyota Prius or Honda Civic, or a conventional plug-in hybrid, but the first "series" hybrid. Instead of a gas engine that drives the wheels along with an electric motor, its small gas engine serves only to keep the lithium-ion battery pack charged. GM's Rob Peterson calls this an "onboard range extender," and it means the car could travel 800 miles between gasoline fill-ups. And it was designed to be affordable. "It's the size of the Chevy Cobalt and will be within range of that price," says GM's Rob Peterson. "We can't offer a $100,000 vehicle to only 5,000 people; we need volume."

Toyota may announce that it is building a plug-in hybrid this year, but if it does so it will be following in General Motors' wake. At the Los Angeles Auto Show late last year, GM chairman and CEO [chief executive officer] Rick Wagoner announced that the company had "begun work on a Saturn Vue plug-in hybrid vehicle." The plug-in technology that the company had once casually dismissed was now a high priority in its product mix.

"This is the beginning of the automakers fulfilling our dreams," says long-term advocate Kramer. Pointing to the first plug-in hybrid from a manufacturer, the DaimlerChrysler Sprinter van, he says, "This is very encouraging, and it absolutely means that carmakers are more likely to put a plug-in hybrid into production." If so, they may be assisted by federal dollars. A bipartisan coalition of 17 U.S. senators and 21 representatives recently sent a letter to President [George W.] Bush asking for $90 million in research funding for plug-in hybrids.

With seesawing gasoline prices and uncertainty about the future of oil, Americans are finally focusing on fuel economy and looking beyond big SUVs [sport utility vehicles] for their next vehicle. A consumer survey by the influential J.D. Power and Associates last summer [in 2006] found that an amazing 57 percent of respondents would consider buying a hybrid car for their next vehicle, and 49 percent would consider a car powered by E85 ethanol. Another survey, by Frost & Sullivan, found that 80 percent are more concerned about fuel prices than they were a year ago. Almost half say they have already bought or would consider buying a more fuel-efficient gas car or hybrid if fuel prices keep going up. And in the sedentary United States, it's impressive that one in five say they're also starting to use alternative transportation: biking, walking, public transportation and car pools.

Despite these numbers—and the fact that cars like the Toyota Prius are proliferating on U.S. roads—hybrids still made up slightly more than one percent of the market in 2006. But by 2013, J.D. Power predicts they'll have taken five percent. This year, expect to see a wide range of new hybrids on the market, from the compact Honda Fit Hybrid (with fuel economy in the mid-50s) to the Toyota Sienna seven-seat minivan (approximately 40 mpg [miles per gallon]). You'll even be able to buy a hybrid version of the Chevy Tahoe (though with only a 25 percent improvement over the SUV's 17 mpg).

After experiencing sticker shock at the pumps, the public is showing interest in a range of cleaner automotive technologies, from hybrids to fuel cells, biodiesel, battery vehicles and plug-in hybrids. Still, consumers remain quite confused about both the potential and the timetable for these technologies, and much of what they think they know is wrong. For instance, it is still commonly believed that hybrid vehicles need to be plugged in. And few are aware that Partial Zero Emission Vehicles (PZEVs) even exist, when they're both affordable and as clean as hybrids in terms of tailpipe exhaust. What's a PZEV, you ask? Read on. Here's a look at some top choices for the environment, and a brief look into the future.

Hybrids

If you buy a hybrid, with both gas and electric motors, you join an exclusive club whose members enjoy tax breaks and entrée into the multi-passenger HOV [high-occupancy vehicle] lanes of California highways—even when they're flying solo. A new group, Hybrid Owners of America, launched last August, has a five-point agenda that includes lifting the cap on the current federal tax break; creating a new tax incentive for owners who convert their hybrids to plug-in status ($15,000 kits are available to do that); a tax break for corporations that "incentivize" their employees to buy hybrids; rewards for automakers that undertake hybrid research; and conversion of 30 percent of the federal car and truck fleet to hybrids over the next three years.

Although hybrid sales slowed somewhat at the end of 2006 as gas prices eased and the federal credit was halved (it went, for example, from $3,150 for the top-selling Toyota Prius to $1,575), 2006 still promised to be the best year yet. By the end of November, 190,966 hybrids had been sold, meaning that 550,000 are on U.S. roads. Some 200,000 hybrids were sold in 2005, doubling the 88,000 sold in 2004.

Other hybrids are on the way. Honda is expected to bring out a 50-mpg hybrid version of its subcompact Fit model in mid-2007. Mazda will produce a hybrid version of the Tribute SUV, which should be mechanically similar to the Ford Escape. The first U.S. hybrid minivan will appear from Toyota this year, a seven-passenger Sienna likely to achieve 40 mpg.

In 2008 and beyond, we will see new hybrids from Toyota (a third generation of the Prius, which, while not a plug-in hybrid, is rumored to have a nine-mile all-electric range), Honda (a new model), Ford (the Fusion), Mercedes[-Benz] (a hybrid "S" Class), Porsche (the Cayenne SUV) and Hyundai. But for immediate gratification, these are the best cars and trucks on the market:

Plug-In Hybrids

While plug-in hybrids remain in the prototype stage, conversion kits are on the market (though availability has been spotty). EDrive's system, with pricing to be announced, replaces the Prius's nickel-metal-hydride battery pack with a larger, lithium-ion pack. Hymotion's kits for the Prius ($9,500) and Ford Escape (as yet unpriced, but definitely more expensive) leave the existing batteries in place but add a lithium-ion auxiliary battery. The drawback is that they're currently available only for fleets. The consumer needs to do research before buying one of these kits, with a particular emphasis on how they affect the car's warranty.

Do plug-in hybrid vehicles simply exchange their pollution source from tailpipe to coal-burning smokestack? It depends on the electric power source, according to a new report released by the American Council for an Energy-Efficient Economy (ACEEE), a nonprofit energy policy group. ACEEE concluded that a plug-in version of the Toyota Prius could reduce CO_2 emissions by a third over a conventional Prius hybrid, but only if its batteries were charged with California electricity—generated mainly from relatively clean sources. In the Midwest, dominated by coal-burning power plants, the report says the plug-in Prius would actually generate one percent more carbon dioxide.

The goal of campaigns like CalCars.org and the nonprofit Plug-In Partners (www.pluginpartners.org), which work with utilities, cities and grassroots groups, is to convince carmakers

The U.S. Ethanol Industry

Over the past decade, farmer-owned and locally-owned ethanol plants have driven the dramatic growth in the U.S. ethanol industry. Of the nation's total ethanol production capacity, about 40% is owned and controlled by U.S. farmers and other local investors. This represents the largest single ownership category in the industry.

The U.S. ethanol industry has increased demand for corn and has played a role in bolstering chronically low corn prices, allowing farmers to earn a modest, market-based profit on their crop. Studies have shown that the local price of corn increases by at least 5–10 per bushel in the area around an ethanol plant, adding significantly to the farm income in the area.

USDA [United States Department of Agriculture] estimates that the Renewable Fuel Standard will generate an additional $2 billion to $4 billion in net farm income by 2012.

American Coalition for Ethanol,
"Ethanol 101," August 2009. www.ethanol.org.

to produce these vehicles on their own. A plug-in hybrid running on ethanol made from sustainably produced switchgrass would be a state-of-the-art clean car, trumped only by a battery or hydrogen-powered vehicle.

Diesel

Diesel vehicles are largely anathema to environmentalists and California clean air regulators, but they're quickly dominating the roads of Europe (where green consciousness is almost a given) and they deserve a second look in the United States, where their numbers can only go up. The good news for diesel partisans is the federally mandated low-sulfur (below 15 parts per million) diesel fuel that went on the market at up to 76,000 American filling stations late last year. It's the cleanest diesel fuel in the world.

One important consideration with diesels is volume: There were nine million diesel vehicles built on the worldwide vehicle market in 2006 (18 percent of the total), but only 300,000 hybrid cars (0.6 percent). By 2010, carmakers will be producing 13 million diesels (and perhaps a million hybrids). If inherently fuel-efficient diesels can reduce our oil dependence without increasing air pollution, Americans need them here. The potential fuel savings with a diesel fleet is 1.4 million barrels of oil a day, about what the United States imports from Saudi Arabia.

The Mercedes E320 BlueTEC is the first diesel vehicle sold in the United States able to take full advantage of low-sulfur fuel. It has a range of 700 miles, and is particularly successful in capturing the nitrogen oxides (NOx) and particulates (with a trap) that are the diesel's Achilles' heel.

Rudy Thom, an environmental affairs research director at Mercedes-Benz, says that BlueTEC is being rolled out in the United States first, because Europe, with 50 percent diesels on the road, still has wildly disparate fuel regulations. The German BlueTEC owner who goes skiing in Italy (where sulfur content is higher) could end up bringing his poisoned car back home on a tow rope.

Biodiesel

There are several forms of biofuel, and the categories can confuse the novice. Biodiesel, in blends with standard diesel of five to 100 percent, has been refined to work without modification in any newer diesel vehicle. With a kit from companies like Greasecar, diesels can burn 100 percent vegetable oil, which can be sourced and filtered from restaurants for a wholly recycled fuel. Biodiesel, which offers both improved emissions and the opportunity to thumb your nose at fossil fuel, is still largely a grassroots enterprise, with enthusiasts banding together in co-ops.

Seventy five million gallons of biodiesel were sold in 2005, but growth of biodiesel, whether made from soybeans or a crop like switchgrass, is limited by our agricultural infrastructure. The National Biodiesel Board, a major booster, nonetheless predicts that under current conditions, biofuels can displace only about 10 percent of current fossil fuel use.

Partial Zero Emission Vehicles

Although they're available on dealer lots in all of the states that embrace the California emission regulations (including Maine, Massachusetts, New York, Connecticut, New Jersey and Vermont, with the likely addition of Washington and Oregon) Partial Zero Emission Vehicles (PZEVs) are largely unknown even to very environmentally aware consumers. There's nothing magical under the hood of a Partial Zero Emission Vehicle (PZEV). It's powered by a gasoline engine, and has a traditional tailpipe emerging from its back end. PZEVs are ultraclean versions of such common vehicles as the Subaru Legacy, Ford Focus and Nissan Altima. They control exhaust gases with sophisticated engine controls and advanced catalytic converters. Although they don't improve on fuel economy, by some measures the emissions from PZEV tailpipes are cleaner than the ambient air. A PZEV *running* is cleaner than a standard car *shut off*, because it emits near-zero evaporative emissions (the gasoline vapors that escape from the fuel system before they reach the engine). All this for at most, a few hundred dollars more than the standard model.

The Future with Batteries and Fuel Cells

If any one technology can replace the internal combustion engine, it's the fuel cell, which doesn't burn anything but converts hydrogen (stored in a tank as liquid or gas) to electricity and its tailpipe emission: water vapor. Fuel cells were invented in the mid-19th century and provided electric power on NASA space missions, but they're only now becoming practical for ground transportation.

The Chevrolet Sequel is one of the world's most advanced fuel cell automobiles, representing many millions of dollars of advanced R&D [research and development]. The Sequel looks like a fairly sleek crossover SUV, but driving it is like nothing else: EVs (fuel cell cars are really electric cars) tend to be slow and plodding, but the Sequel peels out, zooming to 60 mph in only 10 seconds. It seats four with all the creature comforts, including air conditioning, radio and trunk space.

The Sequel is the cutting edge: only two exist. But GM is making 100 of its also-all-new Chevy Equinox fuel cell vehicles available to regular-folk test drivers (in California, Washington, D.C. and Westchester County, New York) this fall. According to Greg Cesul, the company's fuel cell propulsion system chief, these Equinoxes are closely based on the production SUV, and offer the latter's ABS brakes, airbags (or at least room for them), and federal crashworthiness. Redundant safety systems make it very unlikely that a fuel cell car will ever catch fire, let alone explode like the *Hindenburg*.

The Honda FCX fuel cell vehicle is zero emission, fun to drive, has almost 300 miles of range, and is easily refilled at a hydrogen pumping station. So why aren't we driving them yet? Well, the $1 to $2 million price tag is a bit daunting, as is the lack of a hydrogen infrastructure.

EVs show promise, especially with the advent of high-output, lightweight lithium-ion (li-ion) batteries. There haven't been many on the market lately, but San Carlos, California-based Tesla Motors is trying to change that with a snazzy all-electric battery sports car that can achieve zero to 60 [mph] in just four seconds, with a top speed of 130 mph. GM tried the same performance emphasis with its EV1 battery car, but it was limited to about 90 miles of range. If Tesla has been able to achieve both high performance and long range, it's a considerable breakthrough. If not, well, the 100 buyers who just spent $100,000 to sell out the first run of these cars are out of luck.

Even if a practical, affordable hydrogen vehicle appeared tomorrow, it would still be many years before the current fleet went into junkyards. But the rapid acceptance of hybrid cars on the U.S. market is encouraging. America's auto fleet is hardly green, but it's getting greener.

> *"For the foreseeable future, the gasoline engine will stay the predominant power source."*

Gas and Diesel Engines Will Be the Mainstay of the Future

Peter Valdes-Dapena

Despite the hype surrounding gas-electric hybrid and hydrogen fuel cell cars, Peter Valdes-Dapena in the following viewpoint says that the gasoline engine has a long road ahead. Engineers are applying changes to the internal combustion engine, the author maintains, to mimic the high-mileage behavior of diesel engines and electrify automobile systems to further boost fuel economy. On the other hand, he adds that hybrid technology is still complicated and costly, the batteries of electric cars have a limited range, and gas stations are not prepared to fuel hydrogen-powered vehicles. Valdes-Dapena is a staff writer for CNN Money.com.

As you read, consider the following questions:

1. How are engineers looking to improve the inner workings of the internal combustion engine, as described by Valdes-Dapena?

2. According to the author, how does a homogenous charge compression ignition (HCCI) work?

3. What characteristic of batteries limits the electric car's range, in the author's view?

Despite all the hype for electric cars and hydrogen fuel cells, experts say we'd better get used to pumping gas, but we can look forward to much better fuel economy down the road.

"For the foreseeable future, the gasoline engine will stay the predominant power source," said Uwe Grebe, General Motors' executive director for advanced powertrain engineering.

That's because, despite its imperfections, the internal combustion engine has a lot of inherent advantages but plenty of room for improvement. As those improvements are made, future gasoline engines will be more and more fuel efficient, making it tougher for competing technologies to show a big benefit.

Another reason is the fuel itself. Whether we're talking about diesel fuel or gasoline, it's hard to beat hydrocarbons for delivering energy in a potent, easy-to-handle package.

Small non-hybrid gasoline engine cars already get more than 35 miles per gallon on the highway. But only about 15 percent of the energy in gasoline actually makes its way to the wheels, said Fedewa.

That leaves plenty of upside potential, he said.

Gas/electric hybrid technology is a major step in boosting efficiency, but it's complex and expensive. Smaller changes are also squeezing out more of internal combustion's wasted power at lower cost.

Engineers are working on some of the subtler aspects of the engine's inner workings: The timing and spacing of the opening of valves, when and how fuel is injected into the cylinders and when the spark goes off are just some of the things that can be tweaked to extract more motive power from gasoline.

Combining all of these technologies, several car companies are working on something called "homogenous charge compression ignition"—HCCI for short—that allows gasoline engines to mimic the behavior of diesel engines.

In an HCCI engine, gasoline is ignited inside the cylinder using compression and the engine's own heat without the need of a spark. (Spark plugs are still used when the engine is cold.) While there are differences in how the engines work, this is essentially the same way that a diesel engine ignites diesel fuel.

Diesel-powered cars go up to 35 percent farther on a gallon of fuel than similar gasoline-powered cars. The downside of diesels is that they create more pollution, and the exhaust-cleaning technology needed to deal with that pollution is expensive.

That's why HCCI engines seem like an attractive option, provided engineers can get all the bugs worked out. HCCI engines still won't go as far on a gallon as diesel engines, in part because diesel fuel puts out more energy, but they should get about 15 percent better fuel economy than current gasoline engines, said Grebe.

Electrifying Technology

Another process that's already well under way is the "electrification" of more systems within the car. In most cars now on the road, power steering and brakes get a boost from hydraulic pumps or vacuums powered directly by the car's engine. Air-conditioning compressors are also powered directly by the engine.

Many new cars now use electrically assisted power steering and power brakes as well as electrically operated air conditioning compressors. These sorts of systems are an absolute

Clean Diesel

"If you told me 10 years ago that I'd be putting 'clean' and 'diesel' in the same sentence, I'd have said you were out of your mind," says Margo Oge, director of the Office of Transportation and Air Quality at the Environmental Protection Agency [EPA]. However, in response to EPA mandates that went into effect in late 2006, oil refineries are now producing what's called ultra-low sulfur diesel (ULSD). By definition, this "clean diesel" has sulfur concentrations of no more than 15 parts per million (ppm). That's 98.5 percent cleaner than the sludge that coursed through the fuel delivery systems in those disco-era rides, and 97 percent less sulfur than was allowed under a 500-ppm standard instituted in 1993. The cut in sulfur means that less sulfur dioxide goes into the atmosphere, where it can combine with water to produce sulfuric acid—and thus, acid rain. There are further beneficial effects of the sulfur-light fuel, ones that could make the advent of clean diesel as environmentally momentous as the introduction of unleaded gasoline in 1974.

> Ben Hewitt, "The Case for Diesel:
> Clean, Efficient, Fast Cars (Hybrids Beware!),"
> Popular Mechanics, January 2008.
> www.popularmechanics.com.

necessity in gas/electric hybrid cars. Without them, the power steering and brakes as well as the air conditioning would stop working whenever the engine stopped.

Electrification of these accessories could add up to 10 percent of a vehicle's fuel economy said Nick Cappa, an advanced technology spokesman for Chrysler.

The final big step in the electrification of the car will be to remove the gasoline engine from the job of moving the car's wheels. That's the benefit of a so-called range-extended electric vehicle like GM planned Chevrolet Volt.

While the Volt will get enough power to drive 40 miles or so just by plugging into a socket for a few hours, for longer trips extra power would come from a small gasoline engine. The engine would produce electricity that would be stored in a battery to drive the car.

Freeing the engine from directly driving the car has another big benefit. With the engine no longer connected to the wheels, it becomes easier to install entirely different power plants in what is otherwise the same vehicle.

Hydrogen Alternative

That could make vehicles like these the next step to hydrogen fuel cell cars. Both Ford and GM have created range-extended plug-in vehicles with hydrogen fuel cells to generate additional power instead of internal combustion engines.

Hydrogen fuel cells combine hydrogen with oxygen to create water while giving off energy.

The hydrogen fuel cell itself is nearing commercial viability, said GM's Grebe. The problem now is that there isn't much "hydrogen infrastructure" yet. In other words, if you were given a hydrogen fuel cell car today, finding a place to fuel it would be tough.

But talk of pumping hydrogen gas into electric cars brings to mind one of gasoline's big advantages.

The reason range-extended electric vehicles need their ranges extended in the first place has to do with "energy density." That's the amount of energy stored in a given amount of space within the vehicle, including both the fuel and whatever it's kept in.

The low energy density of batteries is what limits the range of electric vehicles. A battery big enough to take a long trip could be as big as the car itself. Compressed hydrogen, including the thick-walled tank needed to store it, is better than a battery.

But it's still not nearly as good as a simple plastic bladder filled with gasoline. If you want to go somewhere far away, there's still nothing better than gas.

At least not for now.

> "The answer to those questioning whether a hybrid will pay off seems to be getting clearer every day."

Gas-Electric Hybrids Are Economic and Fuel-Efficient

Todd Kaho

In the following viewpoint, Todd Kaho proposes that the higher cost of gas-electric hybrids can be offset, keeping in mind several variables. For instance, he uses a straightforward calculation wherein the extra cost pays for itself in savings at the pump after a given number of miles driven, which may be further reduced by government incentives. In addition, the author suggests that hybrids are often outfitted with extra options and trim levels, and have higher resale values than traditional cars. Finally, being an early adopter of green technology is a reward in itself, he claims. Kaho is executive editor of Green Car Journal *and a longtime automotive writer.*

As you read, consider the following questions:

1. What equation does the author use to determine a hybrid's "break-even" point?

Todd Kaho, "Will A Hybrid Car Really Pay Off?" GreenCar.com, June 10, 2008. Reprinted with the permission of GreenCar.com, www.greencar.com.

2. What is the high-occupancy vehicle (HOV) benefit that may come with a hybrid, as described by Kaho?

3. Why should a potential hybrid buyer consider the length of ownership, in Kaho's opinion?

It's true that hybrids cost more than regular vehicles. This prompts many to wonder if the extra cost for these high-efficiency cars is worth it, and in fact if the difference can be offset over time by the cash saved from buying less fuel. While plenty of generalizations have been made on this in recent years, the concept of payback for a hybrid's incremental cost involves many variables and can only be answered on a case-by-case basis. GreenCar[.com]'s research shows that a realistic answer is not so simple and boiling this down into a simple chart is misleading ... so we're not going to do that. Instead, we're going to do this the right way and help you come up with a valid payback factor for the hybrid you may be considering.

You need to know that crunching the numbers involves some elements that are moving targets. For example, higher gasoline prices work to shorten the number of miles needed for payback. Changing government incentives mean that calculations made today may be different than the realities of calculations made a few months down the road. And let's not forget that the retail price of hybrids also appears to be in play as some dealers tack thousands of dollars onto a hybrid's suggested retail price because of high demand.

The Basic Equation

Still, the basic equation for determining a hybrid's break-even point is straightforward. It begins by identifying the combined city/highway mpg [miles per gallon] number for a hybrid and that of its closest conventional counterpart. These mpg figures can be found online at www.fueleconomy.gov. Once armed with these numbers you can figure each vehicle's operating cost per mile based on current fuel prices.

To do so, simply divide the price of fuel (such as $4.00 per gallon) by a vehicle's combined mpg. As an illustration, a Honda Civic Hybrid would pencil out as follows, assuming the above gas cost: $4.00 ÷ 42 mpg = $0.095 (9 ½ cents) per mile operating cost. If a Civic EX was used as a conventional comparison, this would pencil out at $4.00 ÷ 29 mpg = $0.14 (14 cents) per mile. So, the hybrid variant would cost $0.045 (4 ½ cents) less for each mile driven. Placed in these terms, it's enlightening that even at 42 mpg, you're burning nearly a buck's worth of gasoline every 10 miles you drive. Ouch.

Next, determine the manufacturer's suggested retail price (MSRP) for the models you're comparing. The Honda Civic Hybrid MSRP is $22,600 and the standard Civic EX is $18,710, with a differential of $3,890. To find the projected mileage to a break-even point—where the increased fuel efficiency offsets the cost of a hybrid premium—the difference in price between the hybrid model and an identical conventionally powered model is divided by the savings per mile. In the case of the Honda Civic, this figures out this way: $3,890 (cost difference) ÷ $0.045 (4 ½ cents per mile savings) = 86,444 miles. So, at least in theory, the extra cost of a Honda Civic hybrid in this scenario would be offset in just over 86,000 miles of driving if gas prices are $4.00 a gallon.

Of course, federal incentives exist for many hybrid models and this can make a big difference in payback calculations. The Civic Hybrid is currently eligible for a federal tax credit of $1,050, which changes the cost differential between comparative models and results in a payback mileage factor of 63,111 miles if purchased now. However, tax credits are phased out according to specific criteria and disappear when an automaker sells 60,000 hybrids. For example, the Honda tax credit is reduced to $525 on July 1, 2008, and goes away completely on January 1, 2009. The substantial $3,150 tax credit made available for Toyota's Prius when the federal incentive program began has now gone away completely for this model, and in fact all Toyota/Lexus hybrids, because of this automaker's successful hybrid sales. Current information on available credits for specific hybrid models can be found at http://www.fueleconomy.gov/Feg/tax_hybrid.shtml.

These fundamental calculations can be used to determine the theoretical payback for any hybrid model. If the basics are what you're looking for then you're done here. But there are more 'wild card' factors to consider, so if you're inclined to explore how other influences can weigh in, then read on.

Beyond the Basics

If all this sounds simple, rest assured it's not. Finding direct hybrid/gasoline model comparisons can be tricky since many of the features that come standard on hybrid models may not be offered on their gasoline-powered counterparts. Auto manufacturers often sweeten the deal on hybrids with additional content to soften a hybrid's higher price. These extra features cost the manufacturer much less than the added retail value they bring to the consumer, so this content serves to take some of the sting out of the additional money being paid for expensive hybrid technology.

The challenge in identifying a direct hybrid comparison is illustrated by the Toyota Camry. When you add in the engine options and trim levels, Toyota lists 11 different Camry styles and none has the exact mix of options and components as the Camry Hybrid. Also, while a singular example, it should also be noted that Toyota's Prius hybrid has no direct basis for comparison since that body style is offered only as a hybrid.

Still other factors cloud the issue. Driving habits present a significant wild card in this payback equation. Fuel economy can easily differ by 5 mpg or more on high fuel economy vehicles with differences in driving style. Drive with fuel economy in mind and you may well cut the miles to achieving breakeven in half.

Other incentives that influence breakeven are not so obvious, like the ability for solo drivers to use high occupancy vehicle (carpool) lanes in some states. While this incentive can save hundreds of hours of behind-the-wheel time in heavily congested cities over the course of a year—a real quality of life advantage—it also offers tangible financial benefits since cutting commuting time saves fuel, which also saves cash. A case could certainly be made for factoring the dollar value of fuel saved into the payback equation. But again, that's a wild card that must be calculated on a case-by-case basis. Plus, those counting on this must keep in mind that the HOV [high-occupancy vehicle] benefit could go away for new hybrid purchases once quotas are reached, as has happened now in California.

One major consideration when shopping for a new hybrid is the length of time you plan to keep the vehicle. If you're a short-term buyer, then the math to break even may seem impossible to achieve. The big variable here is the resale or residual value when you sell the car. A hybrid will likely retain much of the original premium you paid due to high demand, particularly if you sell it or trade it in after only a few years. So, that $3,000 or $4,000 premium you paid for a hybrid could still add $2,000 or more to the car's value used, meaning you may only need to save $1,000 or so in gas—or consume 250 gallons at $4 per gallon—to hit breakeven.

Finally, there's the subject of battery replacement cost that could (or should) be factored into the equation. While hybrids are new enough so actual battery replacement costs are generally unknown, it's projected that a new battery pack will likely fall in the $2,000 or so range when aging hybrids get to the point where replacement is needed.

Their Own Rewards

When will a hybrid pay for itself? We like to think the day you drive it off the lot. Being an early adopter of environmentally positive technology, reducing oil dependency, and creating less pollution have their own rewards. The substantial savings realized at the pump every time a new hybrid is filled up also provides real and immediate financial gain. With all this and rising gas prices that are already driving up the resale value of efficient smaller cars—a trend that will surely benefit hybrid values as well—the answer to those questioning whether a hybrid will pay off seems to be getting clearer every day.

> *"Hybrids do a far worse job than conventional vehicles in meeting their Environmental Protection Agency fuel economy ratings."*

The Economic and Fuel-Efficiency Claims of Gas-Electric Hybrids Are Exaggerated

Richard Burr

Richard Burr is deputy editor of the Detroit News *editorial page. In the following viewpoint, Burr argues that gas-electric hybrids do not deliver on their highly touted gas savings. When driving under real-world conditions, he claims that the 2004 Toyota Prius fell 42 percent short of its city miles per gallon (MPG) rating and required more refueling than a diesel car. He continues that gas would have to reach over $5 a gallon for years to offset the higher sticker price of the Ford Escape hybrid. Therefore, Burr charges that owning a gas-electric hybrid is merely a fashion statement and should not be subsidized with tax credits.*

As you read, consider the following questions:

1. How was the Toyota Prius outperformed in fuel economy by a Volkswagen Jetta diesel, according to Burr?

2. What are the defenses of hybrid automakers and supporters, as stated by the author?

3. How does Burr support his allegation that tax credits for hybrids benefit the wealthy?

When Treasury Secretary John Snow announced guidelines for a new tax cut for the rich here last week [January 2006], liberals did not denounce him. That's because the proposed tax breaks were for gasoline-electric hybrid vehicles, the favorite ride of environmentalists this side of bicycles. But the dirty secret about hybrids is that, even as the government continues to fuel their growth with tax subsidies, they don't deliver the gas savings they promise.

Most cars and trucks don't achieve the gas mileage they advertise, according to *Consumer Reports*. But hybrids do a far worse job than conventional vehicles in meeting their Environmental Protection Agency [EPA] fuel economy ratings, especially in city driving.

Failing Real-World Tests

Hybrids, which typically claim to get 32 to 60 miles per gallon, ended up delivering an average of 19 miles per gallon less than their EPA ratings under real-world driving conditions (which reflect more stop-and-go traffic and Americans' penchant for heavy accelerating) according to a *Consumer Reports* investigation in October 2005.

For example, a 2004 Toyota Prius got 35 miles per gallon in city driving, off 42 percent from its EPA rating of 60 mpg. The 2003 Honda Civic averaged 26 mpg, off 46 percent from its advertised 48 mpg. And the Ford Escape small sport utility vehicle managed 22 mpg, falling 33 percent short of its 33 mpg rating.

"City traffic is supposed to be the hybrids' strong suit, but their shortfall amounted to a 40 percent deficit on average," *Consumer Reports* said.

The hybrid failed another real-world test in 2004 when a *USA Today* reporter compared a Toyota Prius hybrid with a Volkswagen Jetta diesel, driving both between his home in Ann Arbor, Michigan, and the Washington, D.C., area. Both should have made the 500-mile trip on one tank of gas.

"Jetta lived up to its one-tank billing," reporter David Kiley wrote. "Prius did not."

Kiley had to stop to refill the Prius, which ended up averaging 38 miles per gallon, compared with 44 miles per gallon for the Jetta (which met its fuel economy rating). And this occurred during spring weather without the extra drain on a hybrid battery caused by winter weather—which would have favored the diesel Jetta even more.

Customers complain about the failure to meet fuel savings expectations. There are Web sites such as hybridbuzz.com and chat rooms of hybrid fanatics who bemoan their lackluster fuel economy. About 58 percent of hybrid drivers say they aren't happy with their fuel economy (compared with 27 percent of conventional vehicle drivers), according to CNW Marketing Research in Bandon, Oregon.

It's gotten to the point where Ford is giving hybrid owners special lessons on how to improve fuel economy, according to *USA Today*. They teach drivers how to brake sooner, which helps recharge the battery. But they also drill owners with the same tips that help conventional vehicle owners improve gas mileage: Accelerate slowly. Inflate your tires. Plan your errands better. And this eye-opener: Don't set the air conditioner on maximum. "That prevents the electric motor from engaging," *USA Today* says.

Hybrids are also failing to pay for themselves in gas savings. A study by the car-buying Web site Edmunds.com calculates gasoline would have to cost $5.60 a gallon over five years for a Ford Escape hybrid to break even with the costs of driving a non-hybrid vehicle. The break-even number was $9.60 a gallon for a Honda Civic hybrid.

Hybrid automakers and their supporters have their defenses. They quibble with how some studies are done. They point out that even with their fuel economy shortcomings, hybrids achieve the best gas mileage in three of five vehicle categories rated by *Consumer Reports*. Hybrids are still far lower-polluting than diesels. Their sales are growing fast, even though they make up a small 1 percent of America's annual sales of 17 million vehicles.

Then there's the ultimate defense: They are just like conventional cars because drivers buy them for many reasons other than fuel savings and cost. There's the "prestige of owning such a vehicle," says Dave Hermance, an executive engineer for environmental engineering at Toyota, the leading seller of hybrids. After all, many vehicle purchases are emotional decisions, he says.

A Social Statement

So, hybrids have become the environmental equivalent of driving an Escalade or Mustang. Who cares if they deliver on their promises as long as they make a social statement?

Taxpayers should. The federal government subsidizes hybrid fashion statements with tax breaks that benefit the rich. The average household income of a Civic hybrid owner ranges between $65,000 to $85,000 a year; it's more than $100,000 for the owner of an Accord. The median income of a Toyota Prius owner is $92,000; for a Highlander SUV owner $121,000; and for a luxury Lexus SUV owner it's over $200,000.

This year the government will offer tax credits for hybrid purchases ranging up to $3,400, with owners getting a dollar-

Hybrid Cars Are Losing Efficiency

Consumer Reports road tests found that the 2005 Honda Accord Hybrid saved just 2 miles a gallon (0.7 kilometers a liter) when stacked up against its V6 gas-only counterpart. The hybrid, though, did boast significant performance benefits, such as greater 0-to-60-miles-an-hour (0-to-96-kilometers-an-hour) acceleration.

The buyer's guide rated the Accord Hybrid at 25 miles a gallon (10.6 kilometers a liter), versus the conventional V6's 23 miles a gallon (9.8 kilometers a liter). That's a savings of just under 9 percent.

While such fuel savings aren't negligible, the model is a far cry from the first, superefficient hybrids. The Honda Insight, for example, boasted EPA [Environmental Protection Agency] mileage ratings of 70 miles a gallon (29.8 kilometers a liter) at its 1999 debut.

Brian Handwerk,
"Hybrid Cars Losing Efficiency, Adding Oomph,"
National Geographic News, *August 8, 2005.*

for-dollar benefit on their tax forms. This beats last year's $2,000 tax deduction, which amounted up to a $700 benefit, depending on the driver's tax bracket.

Just a few years ago, liberals criticized the [George W.] Bush administration for allowing professionals to get tax breaks on large SUVs if they were purchased for business purposes. But evidently it's okay to subsidize under-performing hybrids.

Perhaps with more technological advances, hybrids will some day deliver on their fuel economy promise and truly be worth the extra cost. But the tax credits have become just one more welfare program for the wealthy. Let the fast-growing hybrids show that they can pay for themselves.

After all, when Snoop Dogg [American rapper] makes a fashion statement by buying a Chrysler 300 C with a Hemi engine, taxpayers aren't footing part of the bill.

Periodical Bibliography

The following articles have been selected to supplement the diverse views presented in this chapter.

Ty Burr   "Look Ma, No Car!" *Boston Globe*, July 21, 2008.

Csaba Csere   "The Gasoline Engine Still Has a Few Tricks Left," *Car and Driver*, June 2005.

Ben Hewitt   "The Case for Diesel: Clean, Efficient, Fast Cars (Hybrids Beware!)," *Popular Mechanics*, January 2008.

Brendan I. Koerner   "Tank vs. Hybrid: Is It Possible That a HUMMER's Better for the Environment than a Prius Is?" *Slate*, March 18, 2008.

Katharine Mieszkowski   "Electric Cars Are Coming!" *Salon*, May 20, 2009.

Bill Steigerwald   "Scams in Mass Transit," *Pittsburgh Tribune-Review*, October 28, 2006.

Brad Templeton   "Is Green U.S. Mass Transit a Big Myth?" Templetons.com, June 9, 2008.

Ed Wallace   "The Ethanol Lobby: Food vs. Profit," *Business-Week*, May 26, 2009.

Peter Whoriskey   "The Deadly Silence of the Electric Car," *Washington Post*, September 23, 2009.

Mary Wisniewski   "Wave of the Future: Mass Transit," *Chicago Sun-Times*, October 5, 2009.

For Further Discussion

Chapter 1

1. Ted Balaker and Sam Staley argue that perceptions of America's car culture are distorted by myths. In your opinion, does Paul Harris draw on such myths? Cite from the texts to explain your response.

2. Carol Lloyd claims that urban sprawl contributes to obesity. Do you agree or disagree with the author? Explain.

3. Lee Devlin suggests that critics of sport utility vehicles (SUVs) do not look at their carbon footprint in a larger context. In your view, does Stan Cox present a narrow environmental case against SUVs? Use examples from the viewpoints to support your answer.

Chapter 2

1. Brian Tilton asserts that enforcement for seat belts diverts resources. In contrast, Kathryn O'Leary Higgins says that the failure to use seat belts costs taxpayers. In your opinion, who makes the more persuasive argument? Why?

2. Ryan Blitstein insists that the most effective underage drinking and driving laws are comprehensive. In your view, are the laws ScienceDaily supports comprehensive? Explain.

3. Tom Davis writes that graduated licensing programs are difficult to enforce. Do you agree or disagree with Davis? Use examples from the viewpoints to support your response.

Chapter 3

1. Dan Weil claims that proponents of the federal bailout for Chrysler and General Motors rely on lies and misperceptions. In your opinion, are John R. Dabels's reasons for backing the bailout deceptive? Why or why not?

2. Jim Tankersley says that gas-electric hybrids and other green cars will not save the American auto industry. Do you agree or disagree with the author? Use examples from the viewpoints to support your position.

Chapter 4

1. Ryan Avent upholds that mass transit is underfunded. Does Randal O'Toole successfully counter Avent's claim? Explain.

2. Do you agree with the Sierra Club that fuel standards can be raised safely? Use examples from the viewpoints to explain your response.

3. Does Jim Motavalli persuasively address the concern that plug-in hybrids consume electricity from coal-burning sources? Why or why not?

4. Richard Burr alleges that the fuel performance of gas-electric hybrids is exaggerated. In your opinion, does Todd Kaho overstate the benefits of owing a hybrid? Cite from the texts to support your answer.

Organizations to Contact

The editors have compiled the following list of organizations concerned with the issues debated in this book. The descriptions are derived from materials provided by the organizations. All have publications or information available for interested readers. The list was compiled on the date of publication of the present volume; the information provided here may change. Be aware that many organizations take several weeks or longer to respond to inquiries, so allow as much time as possible.

American Beverage Institute (ABI)
1090 Vermont Avenue NW, Suite 800, Washington, DC 20005
(202) 463-7110
Web site: www.abionline.org

The American Beverage Institute (ABI) is an association of restaurant operators that serve alcohol. The institute believes that anti-alcohol activists have gone too far in trying to restrict the consumption of adult beverages. It also believes that current blood alcohol concentration (BAC) limits are ineffective. The association publishes numerous reports on the impact of BAC laws and features a blog on its Web site that addresses current issues surrounding responsible consumption of adult beverages.

American Council for an Energy-Efficient Economy (ACEEE)
529 Fourteenth Street NW, Suite 600, Washington, DC 20045
(202) 507-4000 • fax: (202) 429-2248
e-mail: aceeeinfo@aceee.org
Web site: www.aceee.org

The American Council for an Energy-Efficient Economy (ACEEE) is a nonprofit organization that maintains that energy efficiency and conservation will benefit both the U.S. economy and the environment. The council publishes books and reports on ways to implement greater energy efficiency.

American Petroleum Institute (API)

1220 L Street NW, Washington, DC   20005
(202) 682-8000
Web site: www.api.org

The American Petroleum Institute (API) is a trade association representing America's petroleum industry. Its activities include lobbying, conducting research, and setting technical standards for the petroleum industry. API publishes numerous position papers on transportation-related issues, including papers calling for lower gasoline taxes and fewer restrictions on offshore drilling.

Brookings Institution

1775 Massachusetts Avenue NW, Washington, DC   20036
(202) 797-6000
Web site: www.brookings.edu

The Brookings Institution, founded in 1927, is a think tank that conducts research and education on numerous domestic issues, including automobiles and transportation. Its publications include newsletters, policy briefs, white papers, and books, including *Taking the High Road: A Metropolitan Agenda for Transportation Reform.*

Cato Institute

1000 Massachusetts Avenue NW
Washington, DC   20001-5403
(202) 842-0200 • fax: (202) 842-3490
Web site: www.cato.org

The Cato Institute is a libertarian public policy research foundation dedicated to limiting the role of government and promoting individual liberty. The institute publishes the quarterly magazine *Regulation*, the bimonthly *Cato Policy Report*, and numerous papers dealing with automobiles and transportation in the United States.

Heritage Foundation

214 Massachusetts Avenue NE, Washington, DC   20002-4999
(202) 546-4400 • fax: (202) 546-8328
Web site: www.heritage.org

The Heritage Foundation is a public policy think tank that advocates that the United States must increase domestic oil production. Its publications include the quarterly magazine *Policy Review*, brief *Executive Memorandum* editorials, and the longer *Backgrounder* studies.

International Association for Hydrogen Energy (IAHE)

5794 Fortieth Street SW, Suite 303, Miami, FL   33155
(305) 284-4666
e-mail: info@iahe.org
Web site: www.iahe.org

The International Association for Hydrogen Energy (IAHE) is a group of scientists and engineers professionally involved in the production and use of hydrogen. It sponsors international forums to further its goal of creating an energy system based on hydrogen. The IAHE publishes the monthly *International Journal of Hydrogen Energy*.

National Highway Traffic Safety Administration (NHTSA)

1200 New Jersey Avenue SE, West Building
Washington, DC   20590
(888) 327-4236
Web site: www.nhtsa.dot.gov

The National Highway Traffic Safety Administration (NHTSA) was established by the Highway Safety Act of 1970. It is responsible for reducing deaths, injuries, and economic losses resulting from motor vehicle crashes. This is accomplished by setting and enforcing safety performance standards for motor vehicles, and through grants to state and local governments to enable them to conduct effective local highway safety programs. NHTSA's Web site offers numerous reports, fact sheets, and links concerning automobiles and transportation in the United States.

Natural Resources Defense Council (NRDC)

40 West Twentieth Street, New York, NY   10011
(212) 727-2700
e-mail: nrdcinfo@nrdc.org
Web site: www.nrdc.org

The Natural Resources Defense Council (NRDC) is a non-profit activist group composed of scientists, lawyers, and citizens who work to promote environmentally safe energy sources and protection of the environment. NRDC publishes the quarterly magazine *OnEarth* and hundreds of reports, including "Cleaning Up Today's Dirty Diesels," "Is Hydrogen the Solution?" and "How Biofuels Can Help End America's Oil Dependence."

Reason Foundation

3415 S. Sepulveda Boulevard, Suite 400
Los Angeles, CA   90034
(310) 391-2245
e-mail: feedback@reason.org
Web site: www.reason.org

The Reason Foundation is a research organization that supports less government interference in the lives of Americans. Its libertarian philosophy stands firmly opposed to raising the fuel economy standards of automobiles, arguing that doing so will necessitate smaller cars and thus result in more fatal traffic accidents. The institute publishes the monthly magazine *Reason*.

Renewable Fuels Association (RFA)

1 Massachusetts Avenue NW, Suite 820
Washington, DC   20001
(202) 289-3835 • fax: (202) 289-7519
Web site: www.ethanolrfa.org

The Renewable Fuels Association (RFA) consists of professionals who research, produce, and market renewable fuels, especially alcohol fuels. It also represents the renewable fuels industry before the federal government. RFA publishes the monthly newsletter *Ethanol Report*.

Sierra Club

85 Second Street, Second Floor, San Francisco, CA 94105
(415) 977-5500 • fax: (415) 977-5799
e-mail: information@sierraclub.org
Web site: www.sierraclub.org

The Sierra Club is a grassroots organization that promotes the protection and conservation of natural resources. The organization is opposed to sprawl and the increasing popularity of sport utility vehicles in the United States. It publishes the monthly magazine *Sierra*.

Union of Concerned Scientists (UCS)

2 Brattle Square, Cambridge, MA 02238
(617) 547-5552 • fax: (617) 864-9405
Web site: www.ucsusa.org

The Union of Concerned Scientists (UCS) is a nonprofit alliance of scientists who contend that energy alternatives to oil must be developed to reduce pollution and slow global warming. The union advocates raising the corporate average fuel economy (CAFE) standards, with which automakers must comply, to forty miles per gallon by the year 2012. UCS publishes numerous articles and reports on alternative energy sources and ways to reduce fuel consumption, available on its Web site.

Bibliography of Books

Michael Bender   *The Fast, the Fraudulent & the Fatal: The Dangerous and Dark Side of Illegal Street Racing, Drifting and Modified Cars*. Bloomington, IN: AuthorHouse, 2009.

Lindsay Brooke   *Ford Model T: The Car That Put the World on Wheels*. Minneapolis, MN: Motorbooks, 2008.

Robert Bruegmann   *Sprawl: A Compact History*. Chicago, IL: University of Chicago Press, 2005.

Duncan Clarke   *The Battle for Barrels: Peak Oil Myths & World Oil Futures*. London, UK: Profile Books, 2009.

Kevin Clemens   *The Crooked Mile: Through Peak Oil, Biofuels, Hybrid Cars, and Global Climate Change to Reach a Brighter Future*. Lake Elmo, MN: Demontreville Press, 2009.

Wendell Cox   *War on the Dream: How Anti-Sprawl Policy Threatens the Quality of Life*. Lincoln, NE: iUniverse, 2006.

Robert J. Dewar   *A Savage Factory: An Eyewitness Account of the Auto Industry's Self-Destruction*. Bloomington, IN: AuthorHouse, 2009.

James E. Harbour with James V. Higgins — *Factory Man: How Jim Harbour Discovered Toyota's Quality and Productivity Methods and Helped the U.S. Auto Industry Get Competitive.* Dearborn, MI: Society of Manufacturing Engineers, 2009.

John Heitmann — *The Automobile and American Life.* Jefferson, NC: McFarland & Co., 2009.

William Holstein — *Why GM Matters: Inside the Race to Transform an American Icon.* New York: Walker, 2009.

Charlie Hughes and William Jeanes — *Branding Iron: Branding Lessons from the Meltdown of the US Auto Industry.* Chicago, IL: Racom Communications, 2006.

John A. Jakle and Keith A. Sculle — *Motoring: The Highway Experience in America.* Athens, GA: University of Georgia Press, 2008.

David W. Jones — *Mass Motorization and Mass Transit: An American History and Policy Analysis.* Bloomington, IN: Indiana University Press, 2008.

Brian Ladd — *Autophobia: Love and Hate in the Automotive Age.* Chicago, IL: University of Chicago Press, 2008.

Christopher B. Leinberger — *The Option of Urbanism: Investing in a New American Dream.* Washington, DC: Island Press, 2008.

David Magee   *Crash: Why the Big Three Failed and the Future of America's Automotive Industry*. Lookout Mountain, TN: Jefferson Press, 2009.

Jeff Mapes   *Pedaling Revolution: How Cyclists Are Changing American Cities*. Corvallis, OR: Oregon State University Press, 2009.

Randal O'Toole   *Gridlock: Why We're Stuck in Traffic and What to Do About It*. Washington, DC: Cato Institute, 2010.

Jeremy Packer   *Mobility Without Mayhem: Safety, Cars, and Citizenship*. Durham, NC: Duke University Press, 2008.

Greg Pahl   *Biodiesel: Growing a New Energy Economy*. 2nd Edition. White River Junction, VT: Chelsea Green Publishing, 2008.

Alexander Roy   *The Driver: My Dangerous Pursuit of Speed and Truth in the Outlaw Racing World*. New York: HarperEntertainment, 2007.

Cotten Seiler   *Republic of Drivers: A Cultural History of Automobility in America*. Chicago, IL: University of Chicago Press, 2008.

Daniel Sperling and Deborah Gordon   *Two Billion Cars: Driving Toward Sustainability*. New York: Oxford University Press, 2009.

Christopher
Steiner

$20 Per Gallon: How the Inevitable Rise in the Price of Gasoline Will Change Our Lives for the Better. New York: Grand Central Publishing, 2009.

John Zyrkowski

It's the Sun, Not Your SUV: CO2 Won't Destroy the Earth. South Bend, IN: St. Augustine's Press, 2008.

Index

A

Accidents
car size and, 50–51, 52, 177–178
cell phone use, 68
crash costs, 75–76
crash data, 71–72, 73–74, 87–88, 91, 97, 104
drinking and driving laws and, 85–89, 91–93
fuel economy improvements and, 170
graduated licenses effects, 95–99, 100–106
SUVs, 48, 50–51, 52, 181
Accord Hybrid (Honda), 209
Adaptive cruise control, 164
"Addiction to oil," 19–20, 146
curbing, via fuel efficiency improvements, 167, 168–169, 171, 173, 180
national security issues, 111, 115, 116–117, 167
smoking analogy, 25
Advanced Energy Initiative, 2006, 14
Aerospace industry, 111, 113, 117, 191
Affluent drivers, 53, 208–210
Age of licensure
teen graduated licenses, 95–99, 100–106
U.S. vs. other countries, 86–87
Agriculture and fuel, 27, 188, 190
Air quality
diesel and, 188, 189, 195
improvements despite driving, 28, 31–32
improvements via traffic solutions, 165
Air travel, 63–64
Airline industry, 25, 121
Alcohol Policy Information System, 87–88
American automobile industry
bailout basics, 109–110
history, 125, 132, 143
hybrids and electrics as transformative, 124–134, 182–192
hybrids and electrics not enough to transform, 135–140
job creation, 172–173
must be saved (bailout prostance), 111–117
should not be saved (bailout con- stance), 118–123
SUV/trucks focus, 121, 138
technology leadership, 111, 113–116
See also Hybrid vehicles; SUVs; specific automakers
American Coalition for Ethanol, 188
American Council for an Energy-Efficient Economy, 187
American Public Transportation Association, 157, 160
American Society of Civil Engineers, 149
Anderson, Indiana, 125, 126–127
Appliances, energy standards, 176, 178–179, 180

Atlanta, Georgia, 38, 45

Atwater v. City of Lago Vista
(2001), 79, 80

Auto industry. *See* American automobile industry; European automobile industry; Foreign automakers; Japanese automobile
industry

Auto shows, 116, 184

Avent, Ryan, 145–152

Avoiding Life-Endangering and
Reckless Texting by Drivers Act
(ALERT) (bill), 68–69

Axelsson, Tracey, 57

B

Bailouts, auto industry, 2008-2009,
109–110
    con- stance, 118–123
    pro- stance, 111–117

Balaker, Ted, 28–35

Baltes, Michael, 150

Bankruptcy, car companies
    benefits, 118, 120, 121–122
    Big Three, 24, 109, 125, 136

Battery replacement costs, 203

Battery technology, 183, 184, 187,
191–192, 197–198

Bedard, Patrick, 16

Beetle (Volkswagen), 178

Behind-the-wheel driver training,
100, 101, 105–106

Benefits, costs, 119–120

Bicycle travel
    commutes, 22–23, 58
    health benefits, 36, 37

Big Three. *See* American automobile industry; Chrysler; Ford;
General Motors (GM)

Binge drinking, 90, 92–94
    See also Drinking and driving

Biodiesel, 189–190

Blitstein, Ryan, 90–94

Blood alcohol concentration limits, 85, 88, 89, 91–92

Bloom, Ron, 129

BlueTEC (Mercedes-Benz), 189

Blumenberg, Evelyn, 33

BMW
    328i model, 62
    sales, 137

Bohlin, Nils, 74

Bradsher, Keith, 50, 51, 54

Brand image. *See* Image aspects,
car ownership

Bright Automotive, 124, 125, 127,
134

Burr, Richard, 205–210

Bus travel
    light rail options and, 155,
156, 158–159, 160, 161
    trends, 23

Bush, George W.
    bailouts, auto industry, 2008,
109, 119
    hydrogen fuel cell plans, 14
    oil addiction opinion, 19

C

CAFE standards
    con- stance, 175, 176–181
    history and pro- stance, 166,
167, 170, 172–174
    See also Fuel efficiency stan-
dards

CalCars.org, 183, 187–188

California
    cell phone ban, 68

Global financial crisis, 115
Global warming
  driving decreases as unhelpful, 28, 33–35, 64
  effects, 34
  Kyoto Protocol, 33–34
  mass transit and, 33–35, 145, 147, 152
  SUV emissions among bigger picture, 48, 49, 50, 54–55, 63–65
  SUV/truck emissions as disproportionate, 166, 167–168, 172
Graduated licenses
  may not reduce youth accident rates, 100–106
  reduce youth accident rates, 95–99
Greasecar, 189
Grebe, Uwe, 194, 195, 197
Green cars. *See* Diesel fuel/vehicles; Electric cars; Hybrid vehicles; Hydrogen fuel cell technology; Plug-in hybrids
Greenhouse gas emissions. *See* Emissions standards; Global warming
Grier, Peter, 124–134
Gross domestic product (GDP), 111, 117, 133
Grove, William Robert, 15
Grubb, Willard Thomas, 15

H

Hands-free devices, mobile phones, 68
Handwerk, Brian, 209
Harris, Paul, 21–27

Harvard University
  Kennedy School of Government reports, 152
  School of Public Health College Alcohol Study, 92–93
HCCI. *See* Homogenous charge compression ignition
Health issues, and city planning
  sprawl as unhealthy, 36–42
  sprawl not proven as unhealthy, 43–47
Hermance, Dave, 183, 208
Hewitt, Ben, 196
High and Mighty (Bradsher), 50, 51, 54
High-mileage diesel fuel, 182
High-occupancy lanes, 186, 203
High risk behavior patterns, 72, 73–74
Highways, development and funding
  capacity expansion projects, 162–165
  vs. mass transit, 40–41, 147–148, 149, 151–152, 156–157, 161–162
  state safety law compliance and, 68–69, 92
Holdorf, William J., 82
Home sizes, 32
Homogenous charge compression ignition, 195
Honda
  hybrids, 134, 170–171, 185, 186, 187, 201, 206–207, 208, 209
  hydrogen fuel cell vehicles, 15, 16, 191
Horan, Mike, 103, 105
Horsepower, 131